Table of Contents

INTRODUCTION 7
    POTENTIAL DRAWBACKS AND CONSIDERATIONS 9
INSULIN AND WEIGHT LOSS 11
    MANAGING INSULIN LEVELS FOR WEIGHT LOSS AND HEALTH 13
THE GOLO DIET PLAN 15
SHOPPING LIST 18
RECIPES FOR BREAKFAST 21
    1. Quinoa Breakfast Bowl 22
    2. Berry Smoothie 22
    3. Spinach and Mushroom Scramble 23
    4. Almond Butter Toast 23
    5. Overnight Oats with Berries 24
    6. Avocado Egg Salad 24
    7. Banana Nut Muffins 25
    8. Buckwheat Pancakes 25
    9. Vegetable Frittata 26
    10. Zucchini Breakfast Muffins 26
    11. Fruit Salad with Cinnamon 27
    12. Cottage Cheese with Pineapple 27
    13. Sausage & Veggie Breakfast Skillet 28
    14. Whole Wheat Blueberry Pancakes 28
    15. Spinach and Feta Wrap 29
    16. Apple Cinnamon Oatmeal 29
    17. Baked Eggs with Spinach 30
    18. Almond and Berry Granola 30
    19. Mushroom and Tomato Breakfast Skillet 31
    20. Veggie Breakfast Burrito 31
    21. Turkey and Avocado Wrap 32
    22. Cottage Cheese and Peach Bowl 32
    23. Breakfast Tacos with Salsa 33
    24. Blueberry Protein Pancakes 33
    25. Tofu Scramble with Veggies 34
RECIPES FOR LUNCH 35
    26. Grilled Chicken Salad 36

- 27. Mediterranean Quinoa Salad 36
- 28. Veggie Wrap 37
- 29. Turkey Club Lettuce Wrap 37
- 30. Balsamic Veggie Bowl 38
- 31. Tuna Salad Stuffed Avocado 38
- 32. Grilled Veggie Sandwich 39
- 33. Chicken Caesar Wrap 39
- 34. Caprese Salad 40
- 35. Egg Salad Lettuce Wraps 40
- 36. Shrimp & Veggie Stir Fry 41
- 37. Bean and Veggie Soup 41
- 38. Tomato Basil Soup 42
- 39. Grilled Chicken & Veggie Skewers 42
- 40. Avocado & Tuna Salad 43
- 41. Spinach & Berry Salad 43
- 42. Veggie & Quinoa Stuffed Peppers 44
- 43. Lentil Soup 44
- 44. Grilled Portobello Mushrooms 45
- 45. Tomato & Cucumber Salad 45
- 46. Turkey & Veggie Skillet 46
- 47. Broccoli & Almond Salad 46
- 48. Pesto Chicken Salad 47
- 49. Chickpea Salad 47
- 50. Spinach & Feta Stuffed Chicken 48

RECIPES FOR DINNER 49

- 51. Baked Lemon Herb Chicken 50
- 52. Grilled Steak with Veggies 50
- 53. Garlic Shrimp Zoodle 51
- 54. Spaghetti Squash Primavera 51
- 55. Chicken Fajita Bowl 52
- 56. Grilled Salmon with Asparagus 52
- 57. Lemon Butter Tilapia 53
- 58. Balsamic Glazed Chicken 53
- 59. Eggplant Rollatini 54
- 60. Tofu Stir Fry 54
- 61. Stuffed Acorn Squash 55
- 62. Cauliflower Fried Rice 55
- 63. Grilled Tuna Steaks 56
- 64. Lemon Rosemary Grilled Chicken 56
- 65. Garlic Herb Roasted Vegetables 57
- 66. Stuffed Tomatoes 57
- 67. Turkey Meatballs with Zoodles 58
- 68. Cilantro Lime Chicken 58
- 69. Baked Cod with Veggies 59
- 70. Herb Crusted Pork Tenderloin 59
- 71. Black Bean Stuffed Peppers 60
- 72. Lemon Garlic Roasted Chicken 60
- 73. Balsamic Glazed Salmon 61
- 74. Shrimp & Veggie Sauté 61
- 75. Grilled Eggplant Steaks 62

GOLO DIET FOR BEGINNERS

The Complete Handbook for Sustainable Weight Loss with 2000 Days of Easy, Healthy and Delicious Recipes, Tailored for All Ages, Backed by a 70-Day Meal Plan!

Julia Green

Copyright © 2024

GOLO DIET FOR BEGINNERS

All Right Reserved

RECIPES FOR SWEETS 63

- 76. BAKED APPLE SLICES 64
- 77. BERRY GELATIN 64
- 78. ALMOND BUTTER COOKIES 65
- 79. COCOA-DUSTED ALMONDS 65
- 80. FROZEN BANANA BITES 66
- 81. GREEK YOGURT POPSICLES 66
- 82. DARK CHOCOLATE COVERED STRAWBERRIES 67
- 83. APPLE CINNAMON MUFFINS 67
- 84. VANILLA PUDDING WITH BERRIES 68
- 85. PUMPKIN SPICE MUFFINS 68
- 86. ALMOND FLOUR BROWNIES 69
- 87. COCONUT MACAROONS 69
- 88. BAKED PEARS WITH CINNAMON 70
- 89. COCOA AVOCADO MOUSSE 70
- 90. BANANA ICE CREAM 71
- 91. LEMON POPPY SEED MUFFINS 71
- 92. RASPBERRY ALMOND BARS 72
- 93. BAKED PEACHES 72
- 94. COCONUT & ALMOND CLUSTERS 73
- 95. CHOCOLATE DIPPED ORANGE SLICES 73
- 96. BAKED OATMEAL WITH BERRIES 74
- 97. PINEAPPLE MINT SORBET 74
- 98. BAKED CINNAMON APPLES 75
- 99. CHOCOLATE PROTEIN BALLS 75
- 100. CHOCOLATE-DIPPED BANANA SLICES 76

RECIPES FOR SNACKS 77

- 101. VEGGIE STICKS WITH HUMMUS 78
- 102. ROASTED CHICKPEAS 78
- 103. GREEK YOGURT WITH NUTS 79
- 104. APPLE SLICES WITH ALMOND BUTTER 79
- 105. HARD-BOILED EGGS 80
- 106. SPICED PUMPKIN SEEDS 80
- 107. CHEESE AND ALMOND PLATE 81
- 108. BAKED KALE CHIPS 81
- 109. COTTAGE CHEESE WITH SLICED CUCUMBER 82
- 110. MIXED NUTS 82
- 111. TUNA SALAD ON CELERY STICKS 83
- 112. CHERRY TOMATOES WITH MOZZARELLA 83
- 113. WHOLE GRAIN RICE CAKES WITH AVOCADO 84
- 114. ROASTED SEAWEED SHEETS 84
- 115. CHEESE AND TURKEY ROLL UPS 85
- 116. WHOLE WHEAT PITA WITH TZATZIKI 85
- 117. EDAMAME WITH SEA SALT 86
- 118. WHOLE GRAIN CRACKERS WITH COTTAGE CHEESE 86
- 119. STUFFED MINI BELL PEPPERS 87
- 120. BAKED SWEET POTATO FRIES 87
- 121. CELERY STICKS WITH CREAM CHEESE 88
- 122. CUCUMBER AND TOMATO SALAD 88

123. Trail Mix with Nuts and Seeds	89
124. Apple and Cheese Slices	89
125. Greek Yogurt with Berries and Honey	90

FITNESS GUIDE 91

- The Synergy Between Exercise and the GOLO Diet 92
- Benefits of Physical Exercise in the GOLO Diet 92
- Incorporating Exercise into Your GOLO Diet Plan 93
- Sample Exercise Routine for the GOLO Diet 94

CONVERSION CHART 96

70 DAYS MEAL PLAN 98

CONCLUSION 102

.... 106

"ENJOY THE JOURNEY!" 106

INDEX 107

Introduction

In the constantly changing landscape of dietary and weight management methods, the GOLO diet stands out as a distinct and promising method. Abbreviated as "GO LOse Weight," this nutrition plan prioritizes the maintenance of stable blood sugar levels and has garnered attention for its potential to support weight loss and enhance insulin regulation. Unlike numerous trendy diets that primarily revolve around calorie reduction or the exclusion of entire food categories, the GOLO diet presents a more comprehensive and enduring strategy for attaining health and well-being objectives.

The Origins of the GOLO Diet

Before diving into the specifics of the GOLO diet, it's important to understand its origins and the principles upon which it is built. The GOLO diet was developed by a team of doctors, pharmacists, and nutritionists who sought to create a comprehensive and evidence-based solution to weight management and insulin control.

The core concept behind the GOLO diet is the relationship between blood sugar and weight gain. According to the creators of this diet, unstable blood sugar levels, characterized by spikes and crashes, can lead to increased fat storage and insulin resistance. Insulin, a hormone manufactured by the pancreas, plays a pivotal role in the regulation of blood sugar. When there is a swift increase in blood sugar levels, often triggered by the consumption of high-glycemic foods, the body's response is to release insulin to bring down these elevated levels. Over time, this continuous cycle of spikes and crashes can lead to insulin resistance, where the body's cells become less responsive to insulin's effects, resulting in elevated blood sugar levels.

The Core Principles of the GOLO Diet

The GOLO diet is based on three fundamental principles:

1. **Metabolic Fuel Matrix:** The diet employs a unique Metabolic Fuel Matrix to guide food choices. This matrix categorizes foods into three groups: proteins, carbohydrates, and fats. It emphasizes consuming a balanced combination of these macronutrients to maintain stable blood sugar levels and promote fat burning.

2. **Release Supplement:** The GOLO diet includes a dietary supplement called "Release," which contains a blend of natural components like plant extracts and minerals. This supplement is designed to support insulin management and help regulate blood sugar levels.

3. **Behavioral Changes:** In addition to dietary changes and the use of the Release supplement, the GOLO diet emphasizes behavioral modifications, such as portion control, mindful eating, and regular physical activity. These lifestyle changes are essential for long-term success in weight management and blood sugar control.

Benefits of the GOLO Diet

The GOLO diet has garnered attention for its potential benefits in achieving weight loss and improving insulin management. Some of the key advantages associated with this dietary approach include:

1. **Stable Blood Sugar Levels:** By emphasizing low-glycemic carbohydrates and balanced macronutrient ratios, the GOLO diet aims to keep blood sugar levels stable, reducing the risk of insulin spikes and crashes.

2. **Weight Loss:** Many individuals have reported successful weight loss while following the GOLO diet. The combination of balanced nutrition, portion control, and the Release supplement can contribute to a calorie deficit, which is essential for shedding extra lbs.

3. **Improved Insulin Sensitivity:** The natural components in the Release supplement are believed to support insulin sensitivity, potentially helping those with insulin resistance or prediabetes manage their condition more effectively.

4. **Sustainable Approach:** Unlike extreme and restrictive diets, the GOLO diet promotes sustainable, long-term lifestyle changes. This can lead to lasting results and a reduced likelihood of regaining lost weight.

5. **Focus on Whole Foods:** The diet encourages the consumption of whole, unprocessed foods, which are generally considered healthier options for overall well-being.

6. **Behavioral Changes:** The GOLO diet places a strong emphasis on behavior modification, promoting healthier eating habits and mindful eating, which can benefit individuals in the long run.

Potential Drawbacks and Considerations

While the GOLO diet offers several potential benefits, it's important to consider some of the drawbacks and factors to keep in mind:

1. **Supplement Reliance:** The use of the Release supplement is a core component of the GOLO diet. Some individuals may be uncomfortable with the idea of relying on supplements for weight management and blood sugar control.

2. **Individual Variation:** As with any diet, individual responses can vary. What works for one person may not work as effectively for an extra. It's essential to tailor dietary choices and approaches to one's specific needs and preferences.

3. **Cost:** The cost of the Release supplement and potential long-term use can be a consideration for some individuals.

4. **Complexity:** The GOLO diet's emphasis on macronutrient ratios and the Metabolic Fuel Matrix may be confusing or challenging for some individuals to follow.

5. **Limited Research:** While the GOLO diet has gained popularity, there is still a relatively limited amount of scientific research and clinical trials specifically examining its effectiveness compared to other dietary approaches.

6. **Consultation with Healthcare Professionals:** Individuals with underlying medical conditions or those taking medications should consult with healthcare professionals prior to starting any new dietary plan, including the GOLO diet.

Insulin and Weight Loss

Insulin, a hormone produced by the pancreas, plays a crucial role in the regulation of blood sugar levels within the body. Acting as a sort of key, insulin opens the cellular doors, permitting glucose (sugar) from the bloodstream to enter and present as an energy source. While insulin's primary function is to regulate blood sugar, it has a profound impact on weight gain and weight loss due to its intricate relationship with metabolism and fat storage.

The Role of Insulin in the Body

To understand how insulin influences weight, it's essential to grasp its functions:

1. **Blood Sugar Regulation:** When carbohydrates are ingested, our digestive system processes them into glucose, which then enters the bloodstream. Elevated blood glucose levels signal the pancreas to release insulin. Insulin facilitates the uptake of glucose by cells, helping to reduce blood sugar levels and prevent them from becoming too high.

2. **Fat Storage:** Insulin is also involved in fat metabolism. When insulin levels are elevated, such as after a carbohydrate-rich meal, it promotes the storage of extra glucose as glycogen in the liver and muscles. If glycogen stores are already full, insulin signals the body to convert extra glucose into fat and store it in adipose tissue (fat cells).

3. **Appetite Regulation:** Insulin has the ability to impact appetite and feelings of fullness. Elevated insulin levels can result in heightened hunger and urges for food, potentially leading to overconsumption and weight gain.

The Insulin-Weight Gain Connection

Understanding how imbalances in insulin levels can lead to weight gain and other health problems is crucial for promoting overall well-being. Here are key ways in which insulin contributes to weight gain:

1. **Excess Calorie Storage:** High levels of insulin can lead to the over storage of calories as fat. When insulin remains elevated due to continuous consumption of high-glycemic foods or excessive carbohydrate intake, it promotes the conversion of glucose into fat, leading to weight gain.

2. **Insulin Resistance:** Over an extended period, continuous exposure to elevated levels of insulin can give rise to a condition referred to as insulin resistance. In insulin resistance, cells become less

responsive to the hormone's signals, requiring higher levels of insulin to achieve the same effect. This leads to even more significant fat storage and higher blood sugar levels.

3. **Increased Appetite:** High insulin levels can trigger increased hunger and cravings for sugary and high-carbohydrate foods. This can create a vicious cycle of overeating, further contributing to weight gain.

4. **Fat Accumulation:** Elevated insulin levels promote the storage of fat, especially around the abdominal area. This visceral fat is associated with an increased risk of various health problems, including cardiovascular disease and diabetes.

5. **Metabolic Slowdown:** Chronic high insulin levels can lead to metabolic dysfunction, where the body becomes less efficient at burning calories for energy. This metabolic slowdown can make it harder to lose weight.

Insulin and Weight Loss

While insulin's role in weight gain is well-documented, it's also essential to understand its relationship with weight loss. Proper insulin management is crucial for achieving and maintaining a healthy weight. Here's how insulin influences weight loss:

1. **Balanced Blood Sugar:** To facilitate weight loss, it's essential to maintain balanced blood sugar levels. When blood sugar is stable, insulin levels remain low, and the body is more likely to utilize stored fat for energy.

2. **Fat Burning:** Lower insulin levels encourage the body to switch from using glucose as its primary energy source to burning stored fat. This is a key process in weight loss.

3. **Appetite Control:** Maintaining stable insulin levels can contribute to the control of appetite and the reduction of cravings, making it more manageable to consume fewer calories and adhere to a calorie deficit, a requirement for achieving weight loss.

4. **Improved Insulin Sensitivity:** Engaging in regular physical activity and adopting a balanced diet can improve insulin sensitivity, making it easier for cells to respond to insulin's signals and reduce insulin resistance.

Imbalances in Insulin Levels and Health Problems

Imbalances in insulin levels can lead to a range of health problems beyond weight gain:

1. **Type 2 Diabetes:** One of the most well-known consequences of insulin resistance is the development of type 2 diabetes. In this condition, the body's cells fail to respond adequately to insulin, resulting in elevated blood sugar levels.

2. **Cardiovascular Disease:** High insulin levels can contribute to the development of cardiovascular issues, including hypertension (high blood pressure) and atherosclerosis (hardening and narrowing of arteries). These conditions increase the risk of heart attacks and strokes.

3. **Polycystic Ovary Syndrome (PCOS):** Insulin resistance is often associated with PCOS, a hormonal disorder that affects women's reproductive health. PCOS can lead to weight gain, irregular menstrual cycles, and fertility problems.

4. **Metabolic Syndrome:** A collection of health conditions, which includes high blood pressure, obesity, elevated blood sugar levels, and abnormal cholesterol levels, frequently manifests in individuals with insulin resistance. This amalgamation is referred to as metabolic syndrome and elevates the risk of heart disease, stroke, and the development of type 2 diabetes.

5. **Non-Alcoholic Fatty Liver Disease (NAFLD):** Increased insulin levels can play a role in the buildup of fat in the liver, resulting in NAFLD. If not addressed, this condition can advance to more severe liver disorders.

Managing Insulin Levels for Weight Loss and Health

Achieving and maintaining balanced insulin levels is critical for both weight loss and overall health. Here are some strategies to manage insulin effectively:

1. **Dietary Changes:** Adopt a balanced diet that includes whole, unprocessed foods with an emphasis on complex carbohydrates, lean proteins, and healthy fats. Reduce the consumption of high-glycemic foods, sugary beverages, and processed snacks.

2. **Portion Control:** Be mindful of portion sizes to prevent overconsumption of calories, especially from carbohydrates.

3. **Regular Physical Activity:** Engage in regular exercise, which can improve insulin sensitivity, promote fat loss, and help regulate blood sugar levels.

4. **Stress Management:** Chronic stress can lead to elevated cortisol levels, which can affect insulin sensitivity. Incorporate stress-reduction techniques like meditation, yoga, or deep breathing into your routine.

5. **Adequate Sleep:** Prioritize quality sleep as inadequate sleep can disrupt insulin regulation and increase the risk of insulin resistance.

6. **Medication and Medical Management:** In some cases, healthcare professionals may prescribe medication or insulin therapy to manage insulin levels, especially for individuals with diabetes or severe insulin resistance.

Click to unlock your exclusive bonuses!

🎁 🎁

The GOLO Diet Plan

The GOLO diet plan, is designed to address the underlying causes of weight gain and promote balanced blood sugar levels. It blends specific dietary guidelines, the use of supplements, and behavioral changes to help individuals achieve their weight loss and health goals.

Key Principles of the GOLO Diet Plan

1. Balanced Macronutrient Ratios

The GOLO diet emphasizes balanced macronutrient ratios to maintain stable blood sugar levels and support weight loss.

The typical recommended macronutrient breakdown is approximately 30% protein, 40% carbohydrates, and 30% fat with each meal. This balance helps prevent the rapid spikes and crashes in blood sugar often associated with high-glycemic diets.

- **Proteins:** Lean protein sources such as poultry, fish, tofu, legumes, and lean cuts of meat are encouraged. Protein is essential for maintaining muscle mass, feeling full, and supporting overall health.
- **Carbohydrates:** The focus is on complex carbohydrates with a low glycemic index. These include whole grains, vegetables, and select fruits. Low-glycemic carbohydrates are digested more slowly, leading to gradual increases in blood sugar.
- **Fats:** Healthy fats from sources like avocados, nuts, seeds, and olive oil are recommended. These fats provide essential nutrients and help maintain satiety.

2. The Metabolic Fuel Matrix

The Metabolic Fuel Matrix is a unique feature of the GOLO diet plan that categorizes foods into three groups: proteins, carbohydrates, and fats. This matrix guides food choices to ensure a balanced intake of macronutrients and minimize blood sugar spikes.

3. The Use of the "Release" Supplement

A central component of the GOLO diet plan is the "Release" supplement. This dietary supplement contains a blend of natural components, including plant extracts and minerals like berberine, rhodiola, and inositol.

The Release supplement is designed to support insulin management and help regulate blood sugar levels. Users are typically advised to take this supplement daily as part of their routine.

4. Behavioral Changes

Beyond dietary adjustments, the GOLO diet emphasizes behavioral modifications to promote sustainable weight loss and overall health:

- **Portion Control:** Practicing portion control helps prevent overeating and ensures that individuals do not consume excessive calories.
- **Mindful Eating:** The GOLO diet encourages mindful eating practices, such as savoring each bite, eating slowly, and paying attention to hunger and fullness cues.
- **Regular Physical Activity:** Incorporating exercise into one's routine is essential for overall health and weight management. The GOLO diet encourages regular physical activity, which can further enhance insulin sensitivity and promote weight loss.

The Role of Supplements in the GOLO Diet Plan

The use of the "Release" supplement is a distinctive aspect of the GOLO diet plan. This supplement contains a combination of natural components carefully chosen to support insulin management and help individuals achieve their weight loss & health goals. Let's take a closer look at some of the key components found in the Release supplement:

1. **Berberine:** Berberine is a naturally occurring compound present in a variety of plants such as goldenseal & barberry. It has been the subject of research due to its potential to enhance insulin sensitivity, reduce blood sugar levels, & support weight loss efforts.

2. **Rhodiola:** Rhodiola is an adaptogenic herb that could assist the body in coping with stress and lowering cortisol levels. This reduction in cortisol levels may potentially influence insulin sensitivity and aid in weight management.

3. **Inositol:** Inositol is a vitamin-like compound that plays a role in insulin signaling and may help improve insulin sensitivity in some individuals.

4. **Chromium:** Chromium is a mineral that has been studied for its potential to enhance insulin sensitivity and promote glucose metabolism.

5. **Zinc:** Zinc is a vital mineral that participates in numerous metabolic processes, including the regulation of insulin. Ensuring sufficient zinc intake is crucial for both general health and proper insulin function.

6. **Magnesium:** Another crucial mineral, magnesium, also contributes to insulin sensitivity and the regulation of glucose metabolism.

It's important to note that the Release supplement is meant to complement the dietary and behavioral components of the GOLO diet plan. Users are typically instructed to take the supplement as part of their daily routine to support their weight loss and insulin management goals.

The Phases of the GOLO Diet Plan

The GOLO diet plan is typically divided into different phases, each with its own set of guidelines and objectives. These phases include:

1. **Phase 1 (Kickstart):** This initial phase is crafted to initiate weight loss and establish stability in blood sugar levels. It involves specific dietary recommendations, including the balanced macronutrient ratios and the use of the Release supplement.

2. **Phase 2 (Balancing):** In Phase 2, individuals continue to work on balancing their blood sugar levels and maintaining healthy eating habits. The Release supplement remains a part of the regimen.

3. **Phase 3 (Maintenance):** Once desired weight and blood sugar management goals are achieved, Phase 3 focuses on maintaining these outcomes through a sustainable, long-term approach. This phase places a strong emphasis on behavioral changes, such as portion control and mindful eating, to support lifelong health and weight management.

Shopping List

Proteins

- Skinless chicken breasts
- Lean cuts of beef (e.g., sirloin, tenderloin)
- Turkey breast
- Fish (e.g., salmon, trout, tilapia)
- Lean ground turkey or chicken
- Tofu or tempeh (for vegetarians and vegans)
- Legumes (e.g., lentils, chickpeas, black beans)

Carbohydrates (Low-Glycemic)

- Quinoa
- Brown rice
- Whole wheat pasta (in moderation)
- Oats (steel-cut or rolled)
- Sweet potatoes
- Bulgur
- Barley
- Farro

Fruits (Low-Glycemic)

- Berries (e.g., blueberries, strawberries, raspberries)
- Apples
- Pears
- Cherries
- Plums
- Peaches
- Apricots

Vegetables (Low-Glycemic):

- Leafy greens (e.g., spinach, kale, arugula)
- Broccoli
- Cauliflower
- Brussels sprouts

- Bell peppers (various colors)
- Zucchini
- Cucumbers
- Tomatoes
- Onions
- Garlic
- Carrots

Fats (Healthy Sources)

- Avocado
- Olive oil (extra virgin)
- Nuts (e.g., almonds, walnuts, cashews)
- Seeds (e.g., flaxseeds, chia seeds)
- Nut butter (e.g., almond butter, peanut butter)
- Coconut oil (in moderation)

Dairy and Dairy Alternatives

- Greek yogurt (plain, non-fat or low-fat)
- Unsweetened almond milk or coconut milk (for lactose-free options)
- Cottage cheese (low-fat or fat-free)

Condiments and Spices

- Herbs and spices (e.g., basil, oregano, cinnamon, turmeric)
- Low-sodium soy sauce or tamari
- Vinegar (e.g., balsamic, apple cider)
- Mustard (preferably Dijon)
- Hot sauce (without added sugars)
- Low-sugar salad dressings

Recipes for Breakfast

1. Quinoa Breakfast Bowl

Degree of difficulty: ★★☆☆☆

Preparation time: 10 mins

Cooking time: 15 mins

Servings: 2

Ingredients:

- 1 teacup cooked quinoa
- 1/2 teacup fresh berries (e.g., blueberries, strawberries)
- 2 tbsps severed nuts (e.g., almonds, walnuts)
- 2 tbsps plain Greek yogurt
- 1 tsp honey (elective)
- 1/2 tsp cinnamon

Directions:

1. Cook quinoa using the package guidelines then allow it to cool mildly.

2. Split the cooked quinoa into two containers.

3. Top with fresh berries, severed nuts, and a dollop of Greek yogurt.

4. Spray with honey (if anticipated) and spray with cinnamon.

5. Present and relish!

Per serving: Calories: 240kcal; Fat: 8g; Carbs: 36g; Sugar: 8g; Protein: 9g; Sodium: 15mg; Potassium: 275mg

2. Berry Smoothie

Degree of difficulty: ★☆☆☆☆

Preparation time: 5 mins

Cooking time: 0 mins

Servings: 1

Ingredients:

- 1 teacup unsweetened almond milk
- 1/2 teacup mixed berries (e.g., raspberries, blackberries)
- 1/2 banana
- 1/2 teacup spinach leaves (elective for added nutrients)
- 1 tbsp chia seeds
- Ice cubes (elective)

Directions:

1. Place all components inside a mixer.

2. Blend 'til smooth and creamy.

3. Place ice cubes if you prefer a colder smoothie.

4. Pour into a glass and relish!

Per serving: Calories: 200kcal; Fat: 7g; Carbs: 31g; Sugar: 11g; Protein: 4g; Sodium: 130mg; Potassium: 350mg

3. Spinach and Mushroom Scramble

Degree of difficulty: ★★☆☆☆

Preparation time: 10 mins

Cooking time: 10 mins

Servings: 2

Ingredients:

- 4 big eggs
- 1 teacup fresh spinach, severed
- 1/2 teacup mushrooms, carved
- 1/4 teacup cubed onion
- Salt and pepper as required
- A small amount of olive oil for cooking

Directions:

1. Warm your non-stick griddle in a middling temp. then mildly coat with olive oil.

2. Include cubed onion and mushrooms, sauté till softened.

3. Include severed spinach then cook 'til wilted.

4. Inside your container, whisk collectively eggs, salt, and pepper.

5. Pour your egg solution into your griddle with the veggies.

6. Cook then stir till the eggs are fully cooked.

7. Present hot.

Per serving: Calories: 180kcal; Fat: 12g; Carbs: 6g; Sugar: 2g; Protein: 14g; Sodium: 160mg; Potassium: 360mg

4. Almond Butter Toast

Degree of difficulty: ★☆☆☆☆

Preparation time: 5 mins

Cooking time: 0 mins

Servings: 1

Ingredients:

- 2 slices whole wheat bread (or a suitable whole grain bread)
- 2 tbsps almond butter (no added sugar)
- Sliced banana or berries for topping (elective)

Directions:

1. Toast the whole wheat bread slices.

2. Disperse almond butter uniformly on the toasted bread.

3. Top with carved banana or berries if anticipated.

4. Present and relish!

Per serving: Calories: 300kcal; Fat: 16g; Carbs: 32g; Sugar: 4g; Protein: 10g; Sodium: 220mg; Potassium: 300mg

5. Overnight Oats with Berries

Degree of difficulty: ★★☆☆☆

Preparation time: 5 mins (plus overnight soaking)

Cooking time: 0 mins

Servings: 1

Ingredients:

- 1/2 teacup old-fashioned oats
- 1/2 teacup unsweetened almond milk
- 1/2 teacup mixed berries (e.g., strawberries, blueberries)
- 1 tbsp chia seeds
- 1/2 tsp vanilla extract
- 1/2 tsp cinnamon
- 1/2 tsp honey (elective)

Directions:

1. In a mason jar or container, blend oats, almond milk, chia seeds, vanilla extract, and cinnamon. Stir well.

2. Include the mixed berries on top.

3. Seal the jar and put in the fridge overnight.

4. In the morning, give it a good stir, then include honey if anticipated.

5. Relish your ready-to-eat breakfast!

Per serving: Calories: 320kcal; Fat: 10g; Carbs: 49g; Sugar: 6g; Protein: 9g; Sodium: 80mg; Potassium: 240mg

6. Avocado Egg Salad

Degree of difficulty: ★★☆☆☆

Preparation time: 10 mins

Cooking time: 0 mins

Servings: 2

Ingredients:

- 2 hard-boiled eggs, severed
- 1 ripe avocado, mashed
- 1 tbsp Greek yogurt
- 1/4 teacup cubed red bell pepper
- 2 tbsps severed fresh cilantro or parsley
- Salt and pepper as required
- Juice of 1/2 lime

Directions:

1. Inside your container, blend severed eggs, mashed avocado, Greek yogurt, cubed red bell pepper, and severed cilantro.

2. Blend thoroughly till everything is uniformly incorporated.

3. Flavour using salt, pepper, and lime juice as required.

4. Present as a salad or as a filling for whole wheat wraps or lettuce teacups.

Per serving: Calories: 250kcal; Fat: 18g; Carbs: 11g; Sugar: 2g; Protein: 10g; Sodium: 95mg; Potassium: 540mg

7. Banana Nut Muffins

Degree of difficulty: ★★☆☆☆

Preparation time: 15 mins

Cooking time: 20 mins

Servings: 12

Ingredients:

- 2 ripe bananas, mashed
- 2 eggs
- 1/4 teacup unsweetened almond milk
- 1/4 teacup honey (elective)
- 1 tsp vanilla extract
- 1 1/2 teacups buckwheat flour
- 1/2 teacup severed nuts (e.g., walnuts or almonds)
- 1 tsp baking soda
- 1/2 tsp cinnamon
- A tweak of salt

Directions:

1. Warm up your oven to 350 deg. F then line a muffin tin using paper liners.

2. Inside your blending container, whisk collectively mashed bananas, eggs, almond milk, honey (if using), and vanilla extract.

3. Inside your distinct container, blend buckwheat flour, severed nuts, baking soda, cinnamon, and a tweak of salt.

4. Put your dry components to the wet components and mix 'til just blended.

5. Pour your batter into your muffin teacups, filling each about 2/3 full.

6. Bake for 18-20 mins or for as long as a toothpick that has been placed into the middle emerges out clean.

7. Allow the muffins to cool prior to presenting.

Per serving: Calories: 150kcal; Fat: 6g; Carbs: 23g; Sugar: 8g; Protein: 3g; Sodium: 120mg; Potassium: 150mg

8. Buckwheat Pancakes

Degree of difficulty: ★★★☆☆

Preparation time: 10 mins

Cooking time: 15 mins

Servings: 4 (2 pancakes each)

Ingredients:

- 1 teacup buckwheat flour
- 1 tsp baking powder
- 1/2 tsp cinnamon
- 2 eggs
- 1 teacup unsweetened almond milk
- 1 tbsp honey (elective)
- A small amount of olive oil for cooking

Directions:

1. Inside your container, whisk collectively buckwheat flour, baking powder, and cinnamon.

2. Inside your extra container, beat the eggs and mix in almond milk and honey (if using).

3. Put your wet and dry components and mix 'til just blended.

4. Warm your non-stick griddle or griddle in a middling temp. then mildly oil with olive oil.

5. Pour ¼ teacup of batter onto your griddle for every pancake.

6. Cook 'til bubbles form on the surface, then flip then cook 'til golden brown on both sides.

7. Present.

Per serving: Calories: 220kcal; Fat: 5g; Carbs: 38g; Sugar: 3g; Protein: 8g; Sodium: 230mg; Potassium: 300mg

9. Vegetable Frittata

Degree of difficulty: ★★☆☆

Preparation time: 10 mins

Cooking time: 15 mins

Servings: 4

Ingredients:

- 6 big eggs
- 1/4 teacup cubed red bell pepper
- 1/4 teacup cubed zucchini
- 1/4 teacup cubed onion
- 1/4 teacup cubed tomatoes
- 1/4 teacup severed fresh spinach
- Salt and pepper as required
- A small amount of olive oil for cooking

Directions:

1. Warm up your oven's broiler.

2. Inside your container, whisk collectively eggs, cubed vegetables, and salt and pepper.

3. Warm an oven-safe griddle in a middling temp. then mildly oil with olive oil.

4. Pour your egg solution into your griddle then cook for a couple of mins 'til the edges start to set.

5. Transfer your griddle to the broiler then cook for an extra 5 mins or 'til the frittata is set and mildly golden on top.

6. Slice into wedges and present.

Per serving: Calories: 120kcal; Fat: 7g; Carbs: 5g; Sugar: 2g; Protein: 9g; Sodium: 130mg; Potassium: 240mg

10. Zucchini Breakfast Muffins

Degree of difficulty: ★★☆☆

Preparation time: 15 mins

Cooking time: 20 mins

Servings: 12

Ingredients:

- 2 teacups grated zucchini (about 2 medium zucchinis)
- 2 eggs
- 1/4 teacup unsweetened almond milk
- 1/4 teacup olive oil
- 1/4 teacup honey (elective)
- 1 1/2 teacups buckwheat flour
- 1 tsp baking soda
- 1/2 tsp cinnamon
- A tweak of salt

Directions:

1. Warm up your oven to 350 deg. F then line a muffin tin using paper liners.

2. Inside your container, mix grated zucchini, eggs, almond milk, olive oil, and honey (if using).

3. Inside your distinct container, blend buckwheat flour, baking soda, cinnamon, and a tweak of salt.

4. Put your dry components to the wet components and mix 'til just blended.

5. Split your batter uniformly among your muffin teacups.

6. Bake for 18-20 mins or 'til a toothpick inserted into the center comes out clean.

7. Allow the muffins to cool prior to presenting.

Per serving: Calories: 140kcal; Fat: 6g; Carbs: 20g; Sugar: 6g; Protein: 3g; Sodium: 120mg; Potassium: 180mg

11. Fruit Salad with Cinnamon

Degree of difficulty: ★☆☆☆☆

Preparation time: 10 mins

Cooking time: 0 mins

Servings: 2

Ingredients:

- 2 teacups mixed fresh fruit (e.g., berries, apple slices, orange segments)
- 1/2 tsp ground cinnamon
- 1 tbsp honey (elective)

Directions:

1. Inside your container, blend the mixed fresh fruit.

2. Spray ground cinnamon over the fruit and shake to uniformly coat.

3. Spray with honey if you desire a touch of sweetness.

4. Present instantly as a refreshing fruit salad.

Per serving: Calories: 100kcal; Fat: 0.5g; Carbs: 25g; Sugar: 16g; Protein: 1g; Sodium: 0mg; Potassium: 200mg

12. Cottage Cheese with Pineapple

Degree of difficulty: ★☆☆☆☆

Preparation time: 5 mins

Cooking time: 0 mins

Servings: 2

Ingredients:

- 1 teacup low-fat cottage cheese
- 1 teacup fresh pineapple chunks
- 1/4 tsp vanilla extract
- 1 tbsp severed mint leaves (elective)

Directions:

1. Inside your container, blend cottage cheese, fresh pineapple chunks, and vanilla extract.

2. Garnish using severed mint leaves if anticipated.

3. Present chilled.

Per serving: Calories: 180kcal; Fat: 2g; Carbs: 27g; Sugar: 20g; Protein: 15g; Sodium: 450mg; Potassium: 250mg

13. Sausage & Veggie Breakfast Skillet

Degree of difficulty: ★★☆☆☆

Preparation time: 10 mins

Cooking time: 15 mins

Servings: 2

Ingredients:

- 4 lean chicken or turkey sausages, carved
- 1/2 red bell pepper, cubed
- 1/2 green bell pepper, cubed
- 1/2 onion, cubed
- 1 teacup carved mushrooms
- 2 teacups fresh spinach
- Salt and pepper as required
- A small amount of olive oil for cooking

Directions:

1. Warm your big griddle in your middling temp. then mildly coat with olive oil.

2. Include carved sausages then cook 'til browned then fully cooked.

3. Take out sausages from your griddle then put away.

4. Inside your similar griddle, include cubed bell peppers, onion, and mushrooms. Sauté till softened.

5. Return cooked sausages to your griddle then include fresh spinach. Cook 'til spinach wilts.

6. Flavour using salt and pepper as required.

7. Present hot.

Per serving: Calories: 300kcal; Fat: 12g; Carbs: 18g; Sugar: 7g; Protein: 30g; Sodium: 800mg; Potassium: 700mg

14. Whole Wheat Blueberry Pancakes

Degree of difficulty: ★★☆☆☆

Preparation time: 15 mins

Cooking time: 15 mins

Servings: 4 (2 pancakes each)

Ingredients:

- 1 teacup whole wheat flour
- 2 tsps baking powder
- 1/2 tsp cinnamon
- 1 teacup fresh or frozen blueberries
- 1 teacup unsweetened almond milk
- 2 tbsps honey (elective)
- 1 egg
- A small amount of olive oil for cooking

Directions:

1. Inside your container, whisk collectively whole wheat flour, baking powder, and cinnamon.

2. Inside your distinct container, mix blueberries, almond milk, honey (if using), and egg.

3. Put your wet and dry components and mix 'til just blended.

4. Warm your non-stick griddle or griddle in a middling temp. then mildly oil with olive oil.

5. Pour ¼ teacup of batter onto your griddle for every pancake.

6. Drop a couple of blueberries onto every pancake.

7. Cook 'til bubbles form on the surface, then flip then cook 'til golden brown on both sides.

8. Present with a spray of your honey if anticipated.

Per serving: Calories: 200kcal; Fat: 3g; Carbs: 40g; Sugar: 11g; Protein: 6g; Sodium: 220mg; Potassium: 280mg

15. Spinach and Feta Wrap

Degree of difficulty: ★★☆☆☆

Preparation time: 10 mins

Cooking time: 5 mins

Servings: 2

Ingredients:

- 4 whole wheat tortillas
- 2 teacups fresh spinach leaves
- 1/2 teacup crumbled feta cheese
- 1/4 teacup cubed red bell pepper
- 1/4 teacup cubed cucumber
- 1/4 teacup cubed tomatoes
- 2 tbsps balsamic vinaigrette dressing (low-sugar)

Directions:

1. Lay out the whole wheat tortillas.

2. In the center of each tortilla, layer spinach, feta cheese, cubed red bell pepper, cucumber, and tomatoes.

3. Spray with balsamic vinaigrette dressing.

4. Wrap the sides of your tortilla over the filling, then roll up firmly.

5. Slice each wrap in half diagonally.

6. Present and relish!

Per serving: Calories: 320kcal; Fat: 13g; Carbs: 37g; Sugar: 5g; Protein: 11g; Sodium: 630mg; Potassium: 390mg

16. Apple Cinnamon Oatmeal

Degree of difficulty: ★☆☆☆☆

Preparation time: 10 mins

Cooking time: 5 mins

Servings: 2

Ingredients:

- 1 teacup rolled oats
- 2 teacups unsweetened almond milk
- 1 apple, cubed
- 1/2 tsp ground cinnamon
- 1/4 tsp vanilla extract
- 1 tbsp honey (elective)
- Chopped nuts (e.g., almonds or walnuts) for topping (elective)

Directions:

1. Inside a saucepot, blend rolled oats, almond milk, cubed apple, ground cinnamon, and vanilla extract.

2. Raise to a simmer in a middling temp. then cook for 5 mins, mixing irregularly 'til the oats are cooked then the solution thickens.

3. Sweeten with honey if anticipated and top with severed nuts.

4. Present hot.

Per serving: Calories: 250kcal; Fat: 4g; Carbs: 47g; Sugar: 12g; Protein: 6g; Sodium: 170mg; Potassium: 280mg

17. Baked Eggs with Spinach

Degree of difficulty: ★★☆☆

Preparation time: 10 mins

Cooking time: 15 mins

Servings: 2

Ingredients:

- 4 big eggs
- 2 teacups fresh spinach leaves
- 1/4 teacup cubed tomatoes
- 1/4 teacup cubed onion
- 1/4 teacup cubed bell pepper
- Salt and pepper as required
- A small amount of olive oil for cooking

Directions:

1. Warm up your oven to 350°F.

2. Warm your non-stick griddle in a middling temp. then mildly coat with olive oil.

3. Sauté cubed onion and bell pepper till softened.

4. Include fresh spinach and cubed tomatoes then cook 'til spinach wilts.

5. Split the vegetable solution into two oven-safe ramekins.

6. Crack two eggs into each ramekin.

7. Flavour using salt and pepper as required.

8. Bake in to your warmed up oven for around 15 mins or 'til the eggs are set.

9. Present hot.

Per serving: Calories: 200kcal; Fat: 12g; Carbs: 9g; Sugar: 3g; Protein: 14g; Sodium: 260mg; Potassium: 500mg

18. Almond and Berry Granola

Degree of difficulty: ★★☆☆

Preparation time: 10 mins

Cooking time: 20 mins

Servings: 8

Ingredients:

- 2 teacups old-fashioned oats
- 1/2 teacup carved almonds
- 1/4 teacup unsweetened teared up coconut
- 2 tbsps honey (elective)
- 1/2 teacup mixed berries (e.g., blueberries, raspberries)
- 1/2 tsp vanilla extract

Directions:

1. Warm up your oven to 325 deg. F then line your baking sheet using parchment paper.

2. Inside your container, blend oats, carved almonds, and teared up coconut.

3. Inside your distinct container, mix honey (if using) and vanilla extract.

4. Pour your honey solution over the dry components then stir till well covered.

5. Disperse the solution uniformly on your prepared baking sheet.

6. Bake for 20 mins or 'til golden brown, mixing irregularly to prevent burning.

7. Take out from the oven, allow it to cool, and then stir in mixed berries.

8. Store in an airtight container.

Per serving: Calories: 140kcal; Fat: 8g; Carbs: 16g; Sugar: 4g; Protein: 3g; Sodium: 0mg; Potassium: 90mg

19. Mushroom and Tomato Breakfast Skillet

Degree of difficulty: ★★☆☆

Preparation time: 10 mins

Cooking time: 15 mins

Servings: 2

Ingredients:

- 1 teacup carved mushrooms
- 1 teacup cubed tomatoes
- 1/2 teacup cubed onion
- 2 pieces garlic, crushed
- 1/4 tsp dried thyme
- Salt and pepper as required
- A small amount of olive oil for cooking
- 4 eggs

Directions:

1. Warm your non-stick griddle in a middling temp. then mildly coat with olive oil.

2. Sauté cubed onion and crushed garlic till fragrant.

3. Include carved mushrooms, cubed tomatoes, dried thyme, salt, and pepper. Cook 'til the mushrooms and tomatoes are softened.

4. Create four wells in the vegetable solution and crack an egg into each well.

5. Cover your griddle then cook 'til the eggs are set to your liking (around 5-7 mins for medium-cooked yolks).

6. Present hot.

Per serving: Calories: 180kcal; Fat: 10g; Carbs: 11g; Sugar: 5g; Protein: 14g; Sodium: 170mg; Potassium: 470mg

20. Veggie Breakfast Burrito

Degree of difficulty: ★★★☆☆

Preparation time: 15 mins

Cooking time: 10 mins

Servings: 2

Ingredients:

- 4 whole wheat tortillas
- 4 big eggs, scrambled
- 1/2 teacup cubed bell peppers
- 1/4 teacup cubed onion
- 1/4 teacup cubed tomatoes
- 1/4 teacup cubed avocado
- 1/4 teacup teared up low-fat cheese
- Salt and pepper as required
- A small amount of olive oil for cooking

Directions:

1. Warm your non-stick griddle in a middling temp. then mildly coat with olive oil.

2. Sauté cubed onion and bell peppers till softened.

3. Include scrambled eggs then cook 'til they are almost set.

4. Stir in cubed tomatoes, avocado, and teared up cheese. Cook for an extra min or 'til cheese is dissolved.

5. Flavour using salt and pepper as required.

6. Warm the whole wheat tortillas in a dry griddle or microwave.

7. Spoon the egg and veggie solution onto each of your tortilla, wrap in the sides, then roll up to form a burrito.

8. Present hot.

Per serving: Calories: 330kcal; Fat: 16g; Carbs: 31g; Sugar: 5g; Protein: 17g; Sodium: 400mg; Potassium: 380mg

21. Turkey and Avocado Wrap

Degree of difficulty: ★★☆☆☆

Preparation time: 10 mins

Cooking time: 0 mins

Servings: 2

Ingredients:

- 4 whole wheat tortillas
- 8 slices lean turkey breast
- 1 avocado, carved
- 1/2 teacup teared up lettuce
- 1/4 teacup cubed tomatoes
- 2 tbsps Greek yogurt
- Salt and pepper as required

Directions:

1. Lay out the whole wheat tortillas.

2. On each tortilla, place 2 slices of turkey breast.

3. Top with avocado slices, teared up lettuce, and cubed tomatoes.

4. Spray Greek yogurt over the fillings.

5. Flavour using salt and pepper as required.

6. Wrap the sides of the tortilla over the fillings then roll up to form a wrap.

7. Present instantly.

Per serving: Calories: 350kcal; Fat: 15g; Carbs: 36g; Sugar: 3g; Protein: 24g; Sodium: 650mg; Potassium: 640mg

22. Cottage Cheese and Peach Bowl

Degree of difficulty: ★☆☆☆☆

Preparation time: 5 mins

Cooking time: 0 mins

Servings: 2

Ingredients:

- 2 teacups low-fat cottage cheese
- 2 ripe peaches, carved
- 1/4 teacup severed almonds or walnuts (elective)
- 1 tbsp honey (elective)

Directions:

1. Inside your container, divide the low-fat cottage cheese into two portions.

2. Top each portion with carved peaches.

3. Optionally, spray with severed nuts and spray with honey for added flavor.

4. Present chilled.

Per serving: Calories: 250kcal; Fat: 3g; Carbs: 31g; Sugar: 22g; Protein: 28g; Sodium: 680mg; Potassium: 520mg

23. Breakfast Tacos with Salsa

Degree of difficulty: ★★☆☆

Preparation time: 15 mins

Cooking time: 10 mins

Servings: 2

Ingredients:

- 4 small whole wheat tortillas
- 4 big eggs, scrambled
- 1/2 teacup black beans, that is drained and washed
- 1/2 teacup cubed tomatoes
- 1/4 teacup cubed red onion
- 1/4 teacup severed fresh cilantro
- 1/4 teacup salsa
- Salt and pepper as required

Directions:

1. Warm the whole wheat tortillas in a dry griddle or microwave.

2. Inside your container, scramble the eggs.

3. Fill each tortilla with scrambled eggs, black beans, cubed tomatoes, cubed red onion, and severed cilantro.

4. Top with salsa.

5. Flavour using salt and pepper as required.

6. Present as breakfast tacos.

Per serving: Calories: 320kcal; Fat: 10g; Carbs: 38g; Sugar: 5g; Protein: 19g; Sodium: 680mg; Potassium: 480mg

24. Blueberry Protein Pancakes

Degree of difficulty: ★★☆☆

Preparation time: 15 mins

Cooking time: 10 mins

Servings: 4 (2 pancakes each)

Ingredients:

- 1 teacup old-fashioned oats
- 1 teacup low-fat cottage cheese
- 2 big eggs
- 1 teacup fresh blueberries
- 1 tsp baking powder
- 1/2 tsp vanilla extract
- A small amount of olive oil for cooking

Directions:

1. Inside a mixer, blend old-fashioned oats, low-fat cottage cheese, eggs, baking powder, and vanilla extract. Blend 'til smooth.

2. Gently wrap in fresh blueberries.

3. Warm your non-stick griddle or griddle in a middling temp. then mildly oil with olive oil.

4. Pour ¼ teacup of batter onto your griddle for every pancake.

5. Cook 'til bubbles form on the surface, then flip then cook 'til golden brown on both sides.

6. Present using a spray of honey or a dollop of Greek yogurt if anticipated.

Per serving: Calories: 220kcal; Fat: 6g; Carbs: 25g; Sugar: 6g; Protein: 16g; Sodium: 490mg; Potassium: 260mg

25. Tofu Scramble with Veggies

Degree of difficulty: ★★☆☆☆

Preparation time: 10 mins

Cooking time: 15 mins

Servings: 2

Ingredients:

- 1 block (14 oz) firm tofu, that is crumbled
- 1/2 teacup cubed bell peppers
- 1/2 teacup cubed onion
- 1/2 teacup cubed tomatoes
- 1/2 teacup fresh spinach leaves
- 1/2 tsp turmeric powder (for color)
- Salt and pepper as required
- A small amount of olive oil for cooking

Directions:

1. Warm your non-stick griddle in a middling temp. then mildly coat with olive oil.

2. Sauté cubed onion and bell peppers till softened.

3. Include crumbled tofu then cook for a couple of mins, mixing irregularly.

4. Stir in cubed tomatoes, fresh spinach leaves, turmeric powder, salt, and pepper.

5. Cook 'til the spinach wilts and the tofu is fully heated.

6. Present hot as a tofu scramble.

Per serving: Calories: 180kcal; Fat: 8g; Carbs: 10g; Sugar: 4g; Protein: 17g; Sodium: 330mg; Potassium: 470mg

Recipes for Lunch

26. Grilled Chicken Salad

Degree of difficulty: ★★☆☆
Preparation time: 15 mins
Cooking time: 15 mins
Servings: 2
Ingredients:
- 2 boneless, skinless chicken breasts
- 4 teacups mixed salad greens
- 1 teacup cherry tomatoes, divided
- 1/2 cucumber, carved
- 1/4 red onion, finely carved
- 2 tbsps olive oil
- 2 tbsps balsamic vinegar
- Salt and pepper as required

Directions:
1. Warm up the grill to med-high temp.
2. Flavour the chicken breasts using salt and pepper.
3. Grill the chicken for around 6-8 mins on all sides, or 'til fully cooked and no longer pink in the center.
4. While your chicken is cooking, prepare the salad by combining the mixed greens, cherry tomatoes, cucumber, and red onion in your big container.
5. Inside your small container, whisk collectively the olive oil and balsamic vinegar to make your dressing.
6. Once the chicken is cooked, let it rest for a couple of mins, then slice it into a very thin strip.
7. Split your salad between two plates, top with the carved chicken, and spray with your dressing.
8. Present instantly.

Per serving: Calories: 350kcal; Fat: 17g; Carbs: 12g; Sugar: 5g; Protein: 35g; Sodium: 80mg; Potassium: 600mg

27. Mediterranean Quinoa Salad

Degree of difficulty: ★★☆☆
Preparation time: 15 mins
Cooking time: 15 mins
Servings: 4
Ingredients:
- 1 teacup quinoa, washed
- 2 teacups water
- 1 teacup cucumber, cubed
- 1 teacup cherry tomatoes, divided
- 1/2 teacup red bell pepper, cubed
- 1/4 teacup red onion, finely severed
- 1/4 teacup fresh parsley, severed
- 1/4 teacup feta cheese, crumbled (elective)
- 2 tbsps olive oil
- 2 tbsps lemon juice
- Salt and pepper as required

Directions:

1. In your medium saucepan, blend quinoa and water. Boil, then decrease temp. to low, cover, then simmer for 12-15 mins, or 'til quinoa is cooked and water is immersed. Take out from temp. then allow it to cool.

2. Inside your big container, blend the cooked and cooled quinoa, cucumber, cherry tomatoes, red bell pepper, red onion, and parsley.

3. Inside your small container, whisk collectively the olive oil and lemon juice. Flavour using salt and pepper.

4. Transfer your dressing over the salad and shake to blend.

5. If desired, spray with crumbled feta cheese.

6. Present chilled or at room temp.

Per serving: Calories: 220kcal; Fat: 9g; Carbs: 29g; Sugar: 3g; Protein: 6g; Sodium: 10mg; Potassium: 280mg

28. Veggie Wrap

Degree of difficulty: ★★☆☆☆

Preparation time: 10 mins

Cooking time: 0 mins

Servings: 2

Ingredients:

- 2 whole-grain tortillas
- 1/2 teacup hummus
- 1 teacup mixed salad greens
- 1/2 cucumber, carved
- 1/2 red bell pepper, finely carved
- 1/2 avocado, carved
- 1/4 teacup teared up carrots

Directions:

1. Lay out the tortillas on a clean surface.

2. Disperse hummus uniformly on each tortilla.

3. Place mixed salad greens, cucumber, red bell pepper, avocado, and teared up carrots on top of the hummus.

4. Roll up the tortillas, wrapping in the sides as you go, to create a wrap.

5. Slice in half diagonally, if anticipated.

6. Present instantly.

Per serving: Calories: 330kcal; Fat: 14g; Carbs: 45g; Sugar: 4g; Protein: 8g; Sodium: 320mg; Potassium: 440mg

29. Turkey Club Lettuce Wrap

Degree of difficulty: ★★☆☆☆

Preparation time: 15 mins

Cooking time: 0 mins

Servings: 2

Ingredients:

- 4 big lettuce leaves (such as iceberg or butter lettuce)
- 8 slices lean turkey breast
- 4 slices turkey bacon, cooked and crumbled
- 1 tomato, finely carved
- 1/2 avocado, carved
- 2 tbsps mayonnaise (use a light or reduced-fat version if anticipated)
- Salt and pepper as required

Directions:

1. Lay out the lettuce leaves on a clean surface.

2. Place 2 slices of turkey breast on each lettuce leaf.

3. Top with turkey bacon, tomato slices, and avocado slices.

4. Place a tbsp of mayonnaise on each wrap.

5. Flavour using salt and pepper.

6. Roll up the lettuce leaves to create wraps.

7. Present instantly.

Per serving: Calories: 270kcal; Fat: 16g; Carbs: 8g; Sugar: 2g; Protein: 25g; Sodium: 550mg; Potassium: 440mg

30. Balsamic Veggie Bowl

Degree of difficulty: ★★☆☆☆

Preparation time: 15 mins

Cooking time: 15 mins

Servings: 4

Ingredients:

- 2 teacups cauliflower florets
- 2 teacups broccoli florets
- 2 teacups carved zucchini
- 1 red bell pepper, carved
- 1 yellow bell pepper, carved
- 2 tbsps olive oil
- 2 tbsps balsamic vinegar
- 1 tsp dried Italian seasoning
- Salt and pepper as required

Directions:

1. Warm up the oven to 400°F.

2. Inside your big container, blend cauliflower florets, broccoli florets, zucchini, red bell pepper, and yellow bell pepper.

3. Spray with olive oil and balsamic vinegar. Spray with Italian seasoning, salt, and pepper. Shake to cover the vegetables uniformly.

4. Disperse your vegetables in a single layer on your baking sheet.

5. Roast in to your warmed up oven for 15 mins or 'til the vegetables are soft and mildly caramelized.

6. Present as a side dish or over cooked quinoa or brown rice, if anticipated.

Per serving: Calories: 110kcal; Fat: 7g; Carbs: 12g; Sugar: 5g; Protein: 3g; Sodium: 40mg; Potassium: 460mg

31. Tuna Salad Stuffed Avocado

Degree of difficulty: ★★☆☆☆

Preparation time: 15 mins

Cooking time: 0 mins

Servings: 2

Ingredients:

- 2 ripe avocados
- 1 tin (5 oz) tuna in water, drained
- 2 tbsps Greek yogurt (unsweetened)
- 1/4 teacup cubed cucumber
- 1/4 teacup cubed red bell pepper
- 1 tbsp lemon juice
- Salt and pepper as required
- Fresh parsley or chives for garnish (elective)

Directions:

1. Cut the avocados in half then take out the pits.

2. Inside your container, blend collectively the drained tuna, Greek yogurt, cucumber, red bell pepper, and lemon juice.

3. Flavour the tuna salad using salt and pepper as required.

4. Spoon the tuna salad solution into the avocado halves.

5. Garnish using fresh parsley or chives if anticipated.

6. Present instantly.

Per serving: Calories: 290kcal; Fat: 20g; Carbs: 13g; Sugar: 2g; Protein: 15g; Sodium: 260mg; Potassium: 760mg

32. Grilled Veggie Sandwich

Degree of difficulty: ★★☆☆☆

Preparation time: 15 mins

Cooking time: 10 mins

Servings: 2

Ingredients:

- 4 slices whole wheat bread
- 1 zucchini, carved lengthwise
- 1 red bell pepper, carved
- 1 yellow bell pepper, carved
- 1/2 red onion, carved
- 2 tbsps olive oil
- Salt and pepper as required
- 4 tbsps hummus
- Handful of mixed salad greens

Directions:

1. Warm up a grill or stovetop grill pan in a med-high temp.

2. Brush the zucchini, red bell pepper, yellow bell pepper, and red onion with olive oil. Flavour using salt and pepper.

3. Grill the vegetables for around 4-5 mins on all sides or 'til they are soft and have grill marks.

4. Toast the whole wheat bread slices.

5. Disperse 2 tbsps of your hummus on each slice of bread.

6. Assemble the sandwiches by layering the grilled vegetables and mixed salad greens between the slices of bread.

7. Slice the sandwiches in half and present.

Per serving: Calories: 300kcal; Fat: 13g; Carbs: 39g; Sugar: 9g; Protein: 9g; Sodium: 490mg; Potassium: 620mg

33. Chicken Caesar Wrap

Degree of difficulty: ★★★☆☆

Preparation time: 15 mins

Cooking time: 0 mins

Servings: 2

Ingredients:

- 2 boneless, skinless chicken breasts, that is cooked and carved
- 4 big romaine lettuce leaves
- 4 tbsps Caesar dressing (low-sugar)
- 1/4 teacup grated Parmesan cheese
- Salt and pepper as required
- 2 whole-grain tortillas

Directions:

1. Lay out the whole-grain tortillas on a clean surface.

2. Place 2 romaine lettuce leaves on each tortilla.

3. Split the carved chicken uniformly between the tortillas.

4. Spray 2 tbsps of Caesar dressing over each wrap.

5. Spray with your grated Parmesan cheese.

6. Flavour using salt and pepper.

7. Roll up the tortillas to create wraps.

8. Present instantly.

Per serving: Calories: 350kcal; Fat: 14g; Carbs: 27g; Sugar: 1g; Protein: 31g; Sodium: 790mg; Potassium: 490mg

34. Caprese Salad

Degree of difficulty: ★☆☆☆☆

Preparation time: 10 mins

Cooking time: 0 mins

Servings: 2

Ingredients:

- 2 big tomatoes, carved
- 4 oz fresh mozzarella cheese, carved
- Fresh basil leaves
- 2 tbsps balsamic vinegar
- 2 tbsps olive oil
- Salt and pepper as required

Directions:

1. Organize your tomato slices and mozzarella cheese slices on a plate, alternating them.

2. Tuck fresh basil leaves between your tomato and cheese slices.

3. Inside your small container, whisk collectively balsamic vinegar and olive oil.

4. Transfer the dressing over the salad.

5. Flavour using salt and pepper.

6. Present instantly.

Per serving: Calories: 290kcal; Fat: 24g; Carbs: 6g; Sugar: 4g; Protein: 11g; Sodium: 330mg; Potassium: 420mg

35. Egg Salad Lettuce Wraps

Degree of difficulty: ★★☆☆☆

Preparation time: 15 mins

Cooking time: 10 mins

Servings: 2

Ingredients:

- 4 big lettuce leaves (such as butter lettuce or Romaine)
- 4 hard-boiled eggs, severed
- 2 tbsps Greek yogurt (unsweetened)
- 1 tbsp Dijon mustard
- 1/4 teacup cubed celery
- 1/4 teacup cubed red onion
- Salt and pepper as required
- Paprika for garnish (elective)

Directions:

1. Lay out the lettuce leaves on a clean surface.

2. Inside your container, blend the severed hard-boiled eggs, Greek yogurt, Dijon mustard, cubed celery, and cubed red onion.

3. Blend thoroughly then flavour using salt and pepper as required.

4. Spoon the egg salad solution onto each lettuce leaf.

5. Spray with paprika for garnish if anticipated.

6. Roll up the lettuce leaves to create wraps.

7. Present instantly.

Per serving: Calories: 220kcal; Fat: 14g; Carbs: 5g; Sugar: 2g; Protein: 17g; Sodium: 360mg; Potassium: 250mg

36. Shrimp & Veggie Stir Fry

Degree of difficulty: ★★★☆☆

Preparation time: 15 mins

Cooking time: 10 mins

Servings: 2

Ingredients:

- 8 oz shrimp, skinned and deveined
- 2 teacups mixed stir-fry vegetables (e.g., broccoli, bell peppers, snap peas)
- 2 pieces garlic, crushed
- 2 tbsps low-sodium soy sauce
- 1 tbsp olive oil
- 1/2 tsp ginger, grated
- Salt and pepper as required
- Cooked brown rice (elective)

Directions:

1. Warm olive oil in your big griddle or wok in a med-high temp.

2. Place crushed garlic and grated ginger to your griddle then stir-fry for around 30 seconds till fragrant.

3. Include the shrimp then stir-fry for 2-3 mins or 'til they turn pink and opaque.

4. Include the mixed vegetables then continue to stir-fry for an extra 4-5 mins or 'til the vegetables are soft.

5. Spray low-sodium soy sauce over the stir-fry and shake to blend.

6. Flavour using salt and pepper as required.

7. Present as-is or over cooked brown rice if anticipated.

Per serving: Calories: 180kcal; Fat: 7g; Carbs: 9g; Sugar: 3g; Protein: 19g; Sodium: 520mg; Potassium: 450mg

37. Bean and Veggie Soup

Degree of difficulty: ★★☆☆☆

Preparation time: 15 mins

Cooking time: 20 mins

Servings: 4

Ingredients:

- 1 tin (15 oz) low-sodium black beans, that is drained and washed
- 1 tin (15 oz) low-sodium kidney beans, that is drained and washed
- 1 teacup cubed carrots
- 1 teacup cubed celery
- 1 teacup cubed bell peppers
- 1 teacup cubed zucchini
- 1 onion, severed
- 2 pieces garlic, crushed
- 4 teacups low-sodium vegetable broth
- 1 tsp dried Italian seasoning
- Salt and pepper as required

Directions:

1. Inside your big pot, heat a little olive oil in a middling temp.

2. Include your severed onion and crushed garlic, then sauté for around 2 mins 'til softened.

3. Include cubed carrots, celery, bell peppers, and zucchini to the pot. Cook for 5-7 mins 'til the vegetables start to soften.

4. Pour in your vegetable broth then include the drained and washed black beans & kidney beans.

5. Flavour with dried Italian seasoning, salt, and pepper as required.

6. Boil your soup, then decrease the temp. then let it simmer for 10-15 mins, or 'til the vegetables are soft.

7. Present hot.

Per serving: Calories: 210kcal; Fat: 1g; Carbs: 42g; Sugar: 5g; Protein: 12g; Sodium: 370mg; Potassium: 840mg

38. Tomato Basil Soup

Degree of difficulty: ★★☆☆

Preparation time: 10 mins

Cooking time: 20 mins

Servings: 4

Ingredients:

- 2 tins (14 oz each) cubed tomatoes (no sugar added)
- 1 onion, severed
- 2 pieces garlic, crushed
- 2 teacups low-sodium vegetable broth
- 1/4 teacup fresh basil leaves, severed
- 1/2 teacup Greek yogurt (unsweetened)
- Salt and pepper as required

Directions:

1. Inside your big pot, sauté the severed onion & crushed garlic in olive oil in middling temp. till they become translucent (about 2-3 mins).

2. Include the cubed tomatoes (with its juice) and vegetable broth to the pot.

3. Flavour using salt and pepper as required.

4. Simmer the soup for around 15-20 mins.

5. Take the pot from the heat then stir in the severed fresh basil.

6. Use immersion blender or your regular blender to puree the soup 'til smooth.

7. Return your soup to the pot then stir in the Greek yogurt till well blended.

8. Heat the soup over low heat for a couple of mins 'til it's warmed through.

9. Present hot.

Per serving: Calories: 90kcal; Fat: 2g; Carbs: 15g; Sugar: 8g; Protein: 4g; Sodium: 290mg; Potassium: 550mg

39. Grilled Chicken & Veggie Skewers

Degree of difficulty: ★★★☆

Preparation time: 15 mins

Cooking time: 10 mins

Servings: 2

Ingredients:

- 2 boneless, skinless chicken breasts, that is cut into cubes
- 1 zucchini, carved into rounds
- 1 red bell pepper, cut into chunks
- 1 yellow bell pepper, cut into chunks
- 1/2 red onion, cut into chunks
- 2 tbsps olive oil
- 1 tsp dried Italian seasoning
- Salt and pepper as required
- Wooden skewers (that is soak in water for 30 mins prior to using)

Directions:

1. Warm up a grill or stovetop grill pan in a med-high temp.

2. Inside your container, shake the chicken cubes, zucchini rounds, red bell pepper chunks, yellow bell pepper chunks, and red onion chunks with olive oil and dried Italian seasoning. Flavour using salt and pepper as required.

3. Thread the chicken and vegetables onto the soaked wooden skewers, alternating as desired.

4. Grill the skewers for around 4-5 mins on all sides, or 'til the chicken is fully cooked and the vegetables are soft.

5. Present hot.

Per serving: Calories: 300kcal; Fat: 13g; Carbs: 12g; Sugar: 6g; Protein: 32g; Sodium: 220mg; Potassium: 840mg

40. Avocado & Tuna Salad

Degree of difficulty: ★★☆☆☆

Preparation time: 10 mins

Cooking time: 0 mins

Servings: 2

Ingredients:

- 1 ripe avocado, cubed
- 1 tin (5 oz) tuna in water, drained
- 1/4 teacup cubed cucumber
- 1/4 teacup cubed red bell pepper
- 1/4 teacup cubed red onion
- 2 tbsps fresh lemon juice
- Salt and pepper as required
- Fresh parsley or cilantro for garnish (elective)

Directions:

1. Inside your container, blend the cubed avocado, drained tuna, cubed cucumber, cubed red bell pepper, and cubed red onion.

2. Spray fresh lemon juice over the salad and shake to blend.

3. Flavour using salt and pepper as required.

4. Garnish using fresh parsley or cilantro if anticipated.

5. Present instantly.

Per serving: Calories: 270kcal; Fat: 14g; Carbs: 14g; Sugar: 3g; Protein: 22g; Sodium: 300mg; Potassium: 760mg

41. Spinach & Berry Salad

Degree of difficulty: ★☆☆☆☆

Preparation time: 10 mins

Cooking time: 0 mins

Servings: 2

Ingredients:

- 4 teacups fresh baby spinach
- 1 teacup mixed berries (e.g., strawberries, blueberries, raspberries)
- 1/4 teacup carved almonds
- 2 tbsps balsamic vinaigrette dressing (low-sugar)
- Crumbled feta cheese (elective)
- Salt and pepper as required

Directions:

1. Inside your big container, blend the fresh baby spinach and mixed berries.

2. Spray the balsamic vinaigrette dressing over the salad.

3. Shake to cover the salad with your dressing.

4. Top with carved almonds and crumbled feta cheese, if anticipated.

5. Flavour using salt and pepper as required.

6. Present instantly as a refreshing salad.

Per serving: Calories: 150kcal; Fat: 8g; Carbs: 17g; Sugar: 8g; Protein: 5g; Sodium: 150mg; Potassium: 560mg

42. Veggie & Quinoa Stuffed Peppers

Degree of difficulty: ★★★☆☆
Preparation time: 20 mins
Cooking time: 30 mins
Servings: 4
Ingredients:
- 4 bell peppers
- 1 teacup quinoa, washed and drained
- 2 teacups low-sodium vegetable broth
- 1 teacup cubed tomatoes (tinned or fresh)
- 1 teacup cubed zucchini
- 1 teacup cubed red bell pepper
- 1/2 teacup cubed red onion
- 2 pieces garlic, crushed
- 1 tsp dried Italian seasoning
- Salt and pepper as required
- Grated Parmesan cheese (elective)

Directions:
1. Warm up the oven to 375°F.
2. Cut the tops off the bell peppers then take out the seeds and membranes.
3. Inside your big pot, bring the vegetable broth to a boil. Include quinoa, cover, and simmer for around 12-15 mins, or 'til the quinoa is cooked and the liquid is immersed.
4. In your separate griddle, sauté the cubed zucchini, cubed red bell pepper, cubed red onion, and crushed garlic in your little olive oil in a middling temp. for 5-7 mins, or 'til the vegetables are soft.
5. Stir in the cubed tomatoes, dried Italian seasoning, salt, and pepper. Cook for an extra 2 mins.
6. Blend the cooked quinoa and sautéed vegetable solution inside a container and mix well.
7. Stuff each bell pepper with the quinoa and vegetable solution.
8. Put your filled peppers in your baking dish then cover with foil.
9. Bake in to your warmed up oven for around 20-25 mins, or 'til the peppers are soft.
10. If desired, spray with your grated Parmesan cheese prior to presenting.

Per serving: Calories: 230kcal; Fat: 3g; Carbs: 45g; Sugar: 7g; Protein: 7g; Sodium: 250mg; Potassium: 570mg

43. Lentil Soup

Degree of difficulty: ★★☆☆☆

Preparation time: 10 mins

Cooking time: 30 mins

Servings: 4

Ingredients:

- 1 teacup dried green or brown lentils, that is washed and drained
- 1 onion, severed
- 2 carrots, cubed
- 2 celery stalks, cubed
- 2 pieces garlic, crushed
- 4 teacups low-sodium vegetable broth
- 1 tin (14 oz) cubed tomatoes (no sugar added)
- 1 tsp dried thyme
- Salt and pepper as required

Directions:

1. Inside your big pot, sauté the severed onion, cubed carrots, cubed celery, and crushed garlic in a little olive oil in your middling temp. for around 5 mins 'til the vegetables start to soften.

2. Include the washed lentils, vegetable broth, cubed tomatoes (including the juice), dried thyme, salt, and pepper to the pot.

3. Boil your soup, then decrease the temp. and simmer for around 25-30 mins, or 'til the lentils are soft.

4. Taste and adjust the seasoning as needed.

5. Present hot.

Per serving: Calories: 240kcal; Fat: 1g; Carbs: 46g; Sugar: 5g; Protein: 13g; Sodium: 450mg; Potassium: 800mg

44. Grilled Portobello Mushrooms

Degree of difficulty: ★★☆☆☆

Preparation time: 10 mins

Cooking time: 10 mins

Servings: 2

Ingredients:

- 2 big Portobello mushrooms
- 2 tbsps balsamic vinegar
- 2 tbsps olive oil
- 2 pieces garlic, crushed
- Fresh thyme leaves (elective)
- Salt and pepper as required

Directions:

1. Warm up the grill to med-high temp.

2. Take out the stems from your Portobello mushrooms and carefully clean the caps with a damp paper towel.

3. Inside your small container, whisk collectively balsamic vinegar, olive oil, crushed garlic, fresh thyme leaves, salt, and pepper.

4. Brush the solution over both sides of your Portobello mushroom caps.

5. Grill the mushrooms for around 5 mins on all sides, or 'til they are soft and have grill marks.

6. Present hot as a side dish or on a salad.

Per serving: Calories: 120kcal; Fat: 10g; Carbs: 6g; Sugar: 3g; Protein: 4g; Sodium: 15mg; Potassium: 450mg

45. Tomato & Cucumber Salad

Degree of difficulty: ★☆☆☆☆

Preparation time: 10 mins

Cooking time: 0 mins

Servings: 2

Ingredients:

- 2 big tomatoes, cubed
- 1 cucumber, cubed
- 1/4 red onion, finely carved
- 2 tbsps fresh lemon juice
- 2 tbsps olive oil
- Fresh basil leaves, severed
- Salt and pepper as required

Directions:

1. Inside your big container, blend the cubed tomatoes, cubed cucumber, and finely carved red onion.

2. Inside your small container, whisk collectively fresh lemon juice, olive oil, severed fresh basil leaves, salt, and pepper.

3. Transfer the dressing over the salad and shake to blend.

4. Flavour using additional salt and pepper as required.

5. Present instantly as a refreshing salad.

Per serving: Calories: 120kcal; Fat: 10g; Carbs: 8g; Sugar: 4g; Protein: 2g; Sodium: 10mg; Potassium: 360mg

46. Turkey & Veggie Skillet

Degree of difficulty: ★★☆☆☆

Preparation time: 15 mins

Cooking time: 20 mins

Servings: 4

Ingredients:

- 1 lb. ground turkey
- 2 teacups mixed vegetables (e.g., bell peppers, zucchini, broccoli), cubed
- 1 onion, severed
- 2 pieces garlic, crushed
- 1 tbsp olive oil
- 1 tsp dried Italian seasoning
- Salt and pepper as required

Directions:

1. Inside your big griddle, warm olive oil in a middling temp.

2. Include severed onion and crushed garlic to your griddle. Sauté for around 2 mins 'til they become translucent.

3. Include ground turkey to your griddle then cook, breaking it apart with a spoon, till it's no longer pink then fully cooked.

4. Stir in the mixed vegetables and dried Italian seasoning.

5. Cook for an extra 5-7 mins 'til the vegetables are soft.

6. Flavour using salt and pepper as required.

7. Present hot.

Per serving: Calories: 260kcal; Fat: 11g; Carbs: 10g; Sugar: 3g; Protein: 30g; Sodium: 75mg; Potassium: 460mg

47. Broccoli & Almond Salad

Degree of difficulty: ★☆☆☆☆

Preparation time: 10 mins

Cooking time: 0 mins

Servings: 4

Ingredients:

- 4 teacups broccoli florets, blanched and cooled
- 1/4 teacup carved almonds
- 1/4 teacup dried cranberries (no sugar added)
- 2 tbsps olive oil
- 2 tbsps apple cider vinegar
- 1 tsp honey (elective, for sweetness)
- Salt and pepper as required

Directions:

1. Inside your big container, blend the blanched broccoli florets, carved almonds, and dried cranberries.

2. Inside your small container, whisk collectively olive oil, apple cider vinegar, honey (if using), salt, and pepper.

3. Transfer the dressing over the salad and shake to cover.

4. Flavour using additional salt and pepper as required.

5. Present chilled.

Per serving: Calories: 160kcal; Fat: 11g; Carbs: 14g; Sugar: 5g; Protein: 5g; Sodium: 35mg; Potassium: 340mg

48. Pesto Chicken Salad

Degree of difficulty: ★★☆☆☆

Preparation time: 15 mins

Cooking time: 0 mins

Servings: 2

Ingredients:

- 2 cooked chicken breasts, teared up
- 2 teacups fresh spinach
- 1/4 teacup cherry tomatoes, divided
- 2 tbsps pesto sauce (store-bought or homemade)
- 1 tbsp balsamic vinegar
- Salt and pepper as required
- Pine nuts for garnish (elective)

Directions:

1. Inside your big container, blend the teared up chicken, fresh spinach, and divided cherry tomatoes.

2. Inside your small container, whisk collectively pesto sauce and balsamic vinegar.

3. Transfer the dressing over the salad and shake to cover.

4. Flavour using salt and pepper as required.

5. Garnish using pine nuts if anticipated.

6. Present instantly.

Per serving: Calories: 280kcal; Fat: 14g; Carbs: 6g; Sugar: 2g; Protein: 34g; Sodium: 330mg; Potassium: 780mg

49. Chickpea Salad

Degree of difficulty: ★☆☆☆☆

Preparation time: 10 mins

Cooking time: 0 mins

Servings: 4

Ingredients:

- 2 tins (15 oz each) chickpeas, that is drained and washed
- 1 cucumber, cubed
- 1 bell pepper (any color), cubed
- 1/2 red onion, finely severed
- 1/4 teacup fresh parsley, severed
- 2 tbsps olive oil
- 2 tbsps lemon juice
- Salt and pepper as required

Directions:

1. Inside your big container, blend the chickpeas, cubed cucumber, cubed bell pepper, finely severed red onion, and severed fresh parsley.

2. Inside your small container, whisk collectively olive oil, lemon juice, salt, and pepper.

3. Transfer the dressing over the salad and shake to blend.

4. Flavour using additional salt and pepper as required.

5. Present chilled.

Per serving: Calories: 300kcal; Fat: 9g; Carbs: 44g; Sugar: 9g; Protein: 11g; Sodium: 25mg; Potassium: 450mg

50. Spinach & Feta Stuffed Chicken

Degree of difficulty: ★★★☆☆

Preparation time: 20 mins

Cooking time: 30 mins

Servings: 2

Ingredients:

- 2 boneless, skinless chicken breasts
- 2 teacups fresh spinach leaves
- 1/4 teacup crumbled feta cheese
- 2 pieces garlic, crushed
- 1 tbsp olive oil
- Salt and pepper as required
- Toothpicks (for securing)

Directions:

1. Warm up the oven to 375°F.

2. In your griddle, warm olive oil in a middling temp.

3. Include crushed garlic and sauté for around 30 seconds till fragrant.

4. Include fresh spinach leaves to your griddle then cook for 1-2 mins 'til wilted.

5. Take your griddle from the heat then stir in crumbled feta cheese.

6. Cut a pocket horizontally in each chicken breast, being careful not to cut all the way through.

7. Stuff each chicken breast using the spinach and feta solution.

8. Secure the openings with toothpicks.

9. Flavour the filled chicken breasts using salt and pepper.

10. In an oven-safe griddle or baking dish, sear the filled chicken breasts on both sides in a med-high temp. for 2-3 mins on all sides.

11. Transfer your griddle or baking dish to the warmed up oven then bake for 20-25 mins or 'til the chicken is fully cooked.

12. Take out the toothpicks prior to presenting.

Per serving: Calories: 300kcal; Fat: 13g; Carbs: 3g; Sugar: 1g; Protein: 40g; Sodium: 300mg; Potassium: 650mg

Recipes for Dinner

51. Baked Lemon Herb Chicken

Degree of difficulty: ★★☆☆

Preparation time: 10 mins

Cooking time: 25 mins

Servings: 4

Ingredients:

- 4 boneless, skinless chicken breasts
- 2 tbsps olive oil
- 1 lemon, zested and juiced
- 2 pieces garlic, crushed
- 1 tsp dried thyme
- 1 tsp dried rosemary
- Salt and pepper as required
- Fresh parsley for garnish

Directions:

1. Warm up your oven to 375°F.

2. Inside your small container, blend olive oil, lemon zest, lemon juice, crushed garlic, dried thyme, dried rosemary, salt, and pepper.

3. Put your chicken breasts in your baking dish. Pour your lemon herb solution over the chicken, ensuring they are uniformly covered.

4. Bake in to your warmed up oven for 20-25 mins or 'til the chicken is fully cooked and no longer pink in the center.

5. Garnish using fresh parsley prior to presenting.

Per serving: Calories: 220kcal; Fat: 8g; Carbs: 2g; Sugar: 0g; Protein: 35g; Sodium: 80mg; Potassium: 360mg

52. Grilled Steak with Veggies

Degree of difficulty: ★★☆☆

Preparation time: 15 mins

Cooking time: 10 mins

Servings: 4

Ingredients:

- 4 lean beef steaks (such as sirloin or flank)
- 2 teacups broccoli florets
- 2 teacups bell peppers, carved
- 2 teacups zucchini, carved
- 2 tbsps olive oil
- 1 tsp garlic powder
- Salt and pepper as required
- Fresh herbs for garnish (elective)

Directions:

1. Warm up grill or your grill pan to med-high temp.

2. Flavour the steaks with garlic powder, salt, and pepper.

3. Inside your container, shake the broccoli, bell peppers, and zucchini with your olive oil, salt, and pepper.

4. Grill your steaks for around 4-5 mins on all sides for medium-rare (adjust cooking time to your preference).

5. During the last 5 mins of grilling the steaks, include the seasoned vegetables to the grill then cook 'til they are soft and have grill marks.

6. Take the steaks and vegetables from the grill, let the meat rest for a couple of mins, then slice it finely.

7. Present the carved steak with grilled vegetables, garnished with fresh herbs if anticipated.

Per serving: Calories: 280kcal; Fat: 12g; Carbs: 10g; Sugar: 4g; Protein: 34g; Sodium: 75mg; Potassium: 850mg

53. Garlic Shrimp Zoodle

Degree of difficulty: ★★☆☆☆

Preparation time: 15 mins

Cooking time: 10 mins

Servings: 4

Ingredients:

- 1 lb. big shrimp, skinned and deveined
- 4 medium zucchinis, spiralized into zoodles
- 2 tbsps olive oil
- 4 pieces garlic, crushed
- 1 tsp red pepper flakes (elective)
- Salt and pepper as required
- Fresh parsley for garnish

Directions:

1. Warm olive oil in your big griddle in a middling temp. Place crushed garlic and red pepper flakes (if using) and sauté for around 1 min till fragrant.

2. Include the shrimp to your griddle then cook for 2-3 mins on each side 'til pink and opaque. Take out the cooked shrimp from your griddle then put away.

3. Inside your similar griddle, include the zucchini zoodles and sauté for 2-3 mins 'til they are mildly soft but still crisp.

4. Return your cooked shrimp to your griddle with the zoodles, and shake everything together to blend. Flavour using salt and pepper as required.

5. Garnish using fresh parsley and present.

Per serving: Calories: 180kcal; Fat: 7g; Carbs: 6g; Sugar: 3g; Protein: 23g; Sodium: 200mg; Potassium: 550mg

54. Spaghetti Squash Primavera

Degree of difficulty: ★★☆☆☆

Preparation time: 15 mins

Cooking time: 45 mins

Servings: 4

Ingredients:

- 1 medium spaghetti squash
- 2 tbsps olive oil
- 1 small onion, cubed
- 2 pieces garlic, crushed
- 2 teacups cherry tomatoes, divided
- 2 teacups broccoli florets
- 1 teacup carved mushrooms
- 1 tsp dried Italian seasoning
- Salt and pepper as required
- Fresh basil for garnish (elective)

Directions:

1. Warm up your oven to 375°F.

2. Cut your spaghetti squash in half lengthwise then take out the seeds. Put your squash halves cut side down on your baking sheet and roast for 35-45 mins, or 'til the flesh can simply be scraped into "spaghetti" strands with a fork.

3. While your squash is roasting, warm olive oil in your big griddle in a middling temp. Include cubed onion and crushed garlic and sauté for 2-3 mins 'til softened.

4. Include cherry tomatoes, broccoli, mushrooms, Italian seasoning, salt, and pepper to your griddle. Sauté for an extra 5-7 mins 'til the vegetables are soft.

5. Once the spaghetti squash is done, scrape the flesh into strands using a fork. Include the spaghetti squash to your griddle with the sautéed vegetables and shake everything together to blend.

6. Garnish using fresh basil if anticipated and present.

Per serving: Calories: 110kcal; Fat: 7g; Carbs: 14g; Sugar: 5g; Protein: 2g; Sodium: 45mg; Potassium: 420mg

55. Chicken Fajita Bowl

Degree of difficulty: ★★★☆☆
Preparation time: 20 mins
Cooking time: 15 mins
Servings: 4
Ingredients:
- 1 lb. boneless, that is skinless chicken breasts, carved into strips
- 1 tbsp olive oil
- 1 bell pepper, carved
- 1 onion, carved
- 1 tsp chili powder
- 1 tsp cumin
- 1/2 tsp paprika
- Salt and pepper as required
- 2 teacups cauliflower rice (store-bought or homemade)
- 1 teacup black beans, that is drained and washed
- 1 teacup cubed tomatoes (tinned or fresh)
- Fresh cilantro for garnish (elective)
- Sliced avocado for garnish (elective)
- Lime wedges for garnish (elective)

Directions:
1. Warm olive oil in your big griddle in a med-high temp. Include chicken strips then cook for 5-7 mins 'til they are no longer pink in the center. Take out from your griddle then put away.
2. Inside your similar griddle, include carved bell pepper and onion. Sauté for 5-7 mins 'til they are soft and mildly caramelized.
3. Include chili powder, cumin, paprika, salt, and pepper to your griddle with the sautéed vegetables. Stir to cover.
4. Include cauliflower rice to your griddle then cook for 3-5 mins, mixing irregularly, till it's fully heated.
5. To assemble the containers, divide the cauliflower rice solution among four containers. Top with cooked chicken, black beans, and cubed tomatoes.
6. Garnish using fresh cilantro, carved avocado, and lime wedges if anticipated.

Per serving: Calories: 290kcal; Fat: 8g; Carbs: 21g; Sugar: 4g; Protein: 32g; Sodium: 480mg; Potassium: 650mg

56. Grilled Salmon with Asparagus

Degree of difficulty: ★★☆☆☆

Preparation time: 10 mins

Cooking time: 15 mins

Servings: 4

Ingredients:

- 4 salmon fillets
- 1 bunch asparagus, clipped
- 2 tbsps olive oil
- 2 pieces garlic, crushed
- Juice of 1 lemon
- Salt and pepper as required
- Fresh dill for garnish (elective)

Directions:

1. Warm up your grill to med-high temp.

2. Inside your container, whisk collectively olive oil, crushed garlic, lemon juice, salt, and pepper.

3. Brush the salmon fillets and asparagus with the olive oil solution.

4. Grill the salmon for around 4-5 mins on all sides or 'til it flakes simply with a fork. Grill the asparagus for around 5-7 mins 'til soft.

5. Take out from the grill, garnish with fresh dill (if anticipated), and present.

Per serving: Calories: 280kcal; Fat: 15g; Carbs: 4g; Sugar: 2g; Protein: 31g; Sodium: 80mg; Potassium: 850mg

57. Lemon Butter Tilapia

Degree of difficulty: ★★☆☆☆

Preparation time: 10 mins

Cooking time: 10 mins

Servings: 4

Ingredients:

- 4 tilapia fillets
- 2 tbsps unsalted butter
- 2 pieces garlic, crushed
- Juice of 1 lemon
- Zest of 1 lemon
- Salt and pepper as required
- Fresh parsley for garnish (elective)

Directions:

1. In your griddle, dissolve the butter in a med-high temp.

2. Include crushed garlic and sauté for around 1 min till fragrant.

3. Flavour the tilapia fillets using salt and pepper and put them in your griddle.

4. Cook the tilapia for around 2-3 mins on all sides till it's opaque and flakes simply.

5. Pour lemon juice and zest over the cooked tilapia, then take out from temp..

6. Garnish using fresh parsley (if anticipated) and present.

Per serving: Calories: 150kcal; Fat: 7g; Carbs: 2g; Sugar: 0g; Protein: 21g; Sodium: 80mg; Potassium: 330mg

58. Balsamic Glazed Chicken

Degree of difficulty: ★★☆☆☆

Preparation time: 10 mins

Cooking time: 20 mins

Servings: 4

Ingredients:

- 4 boneless, skinless chicken breasts
- 1/4 teacup balsamic vinegar
- 2 tbsps olive oil
- 2 pieces garlic, crushed
- 2 tbsps honey (elective, for a touch of sweetness)
- Salt and pepper as required
- Fresh basil for garnish (elective)

Directions:

1. Inside your container, whisk collectively balsamic vinegar, olive oil, crushed garlic, honey (if using), salt, and pepper.

2. Put your chicken breasts in your resealable plastic bag then pour the balsamic solution over them. Seal your bag then marinate in the fridge for almost 15 mins.

3. Warm up grill or your grill pan to med-high temp.

4. Grill the chicken for around 6-7 mins on all sides or 'til it's fully cooked and no longer pink in the center.

5. Take out from the grill, garnish with fresh basil (if anticipated), and present.

Per serving: Calories: 220kcal; Fat: 8g; Carbs: 4g; Sugar: 3g; Protein: 30g; Sodium: 75mg; Potassium: 430mg

59. Eggplant Rollatini

Degree of difficulty: ★★★☆☆
Preparation time: 20 mins
Cooking time: 30 mins
Servings: 4
Ingredients:
- 1 big eggplant, finely carved lengthwise
- 1 teacup part-skim ricotta cheese
- 1/4 teacup grated Parmesan cheese
- 1 egg
- 2 teacups marinara sauce (low-sugar)
- 1 teacup teared up mozzarella cheese
- Fresh basil for garnish (elective)
- Olive oil for brushing

Directions:
1. Warm up your oven to 375°F.
2. Brush your eggplant slices using olive oil then grill them for around 2 mins on all sides till they are soft and have grill marks. Alternatively, you can bake them in your oven for around 10 mins on each side.
3. Inside your container, blend ricotta cheese, grated Parmesan cheese, and the egg. Blend thoroughly.
4. Disperse a spoonful of your ricotta solution onto each grilled eggplant slice, then roll them up.
5. Disperse thin layer of your marinara sauce on the bottom of your baking dish.
6. Put your eggplant rolls in the baking dish, seam side down.
7. Pour your remaining marinara sauce over the eggplant rolls and top with teared up mozzarella cheese.
8. Bake in to your warmed up oven for around 20 mins, or 'til the cheese is bubbly and golden.
9. Garnish using fresh basil (if anticipated) and present.

Per serving: Calories: 270kcal; Fat: 15g; Carbs: 18g; Sugar: 8g; Protein: 16g; Sodium: 670mg; Potassium: 500mg

60. Tofu Stir Fry

Degree of difficulty: ★★☆☆☆
Preparation time: 15 mins
Cooking time: 15 mins
Servings: 4
Ingredients:
- 1 block firm tofu, cubed
- 2 tbsps low-sodium soy sauce
- 1 tbsp sesame oil
- 2 pieces garlic, crushed
- 1-inch piece of ginger, crushed
- 1 red bell pepper, carved
- 1 yellow bell pepper, carved
- 1 teacup broccoli florets
- 1 teacup snap peas
- 2 carrots, julienned
- 2 tbsps severed scallions (green parts)
- Sesame seeds for garnish (elective)

Directions:
1. Inside your small container, blend collectively soy sauce, sesame oil, crushed garlic, and crushed ginger.
2. Press tofu to take out extra moisture, then cut it into cubes.
3. Warm your big griddle or wok in a med-high temp. Include the cubed tofu then stir-fry till it's mildly browned on all sides.
4. Take out the tofu from your griddle then put it away.
5. Inside your similar griddle, include a bit more sesame oil if needed, then stir-fry the bell peppers, broccoli, snap peas, and carrots for 5-7 mins, or 'til they are soft-crisp.
6. Return your tofu to your griddle then pour the sauce over the tofu and vegetables. Stir-fry for an extra 2-3 mins 'til everything is covered in the sauce.
7. Spray with severed scallions and sesame seeds (if anticipated).
8. Present.

Per serving: Calories: 180kcal; Fat: 10g; Carbs: 14g; Sugar: 6g; Protein: 12g; Sodium: 370mg; Potassium: 460mg

61. Stuffed Acorn Squash

Degree of difficulty: ★★★☆☆
Preparation time: 20 mins
Cooking time: 40 mins
Servings: 4
Ingredients:

- 2 acorn squash, divided and seeds taken out
- 1 teacup quinoa, cooked
- 1 teacup lean ground turkey or chicken
- 1 small onion, severed
- 1 bell pepper, severed
- 2 pieces garlic, crushed
- 1 tsp dried thyme
- Salt and pepper as required
- Olive oil for drizzling

Directions:

1. Warm up your oven to 375°F.

2. Put your divided acorn squash on your baking sheet, cut side up. Spray using a little olive oil then flavour using salt and pepper. Roast for around 30-40 mins or 'til the squash is soft.

3. While squash is roasting, prepare the filling. In your griddle, cook the ground turkey or chicken in a middling temp. till it's no longer pink. Take out from your griddle then put away.

4. Inside your similar griddle, include a bit more olive oil if needed. Sauté the severed onion, bell pepper, and garlic till they are softened.

5. Stir in the cooked quinoa, cooked ground turkey or chicken, dried thyme, salt, and pepper. Blend thoroughly and heat through.

6. Once the acorn squash halves are done roasting, fill each half with the quinoa and turkey/chicken solution.

7. Put your filled squash back in your oven for an extra 5-10 mins to heat through.

8. Present and relish!

Per serving: Calories: 350kcal; Fat: 7g; Carbs: 54g; Sugar: 4g; Protein: 21g; Sodium: 70mg; Potassium: 1010mg

62. Cauliflower Fried Rice

Degree of difficulty: ★★☆☆☆
Preparation time: 15 mins
Cooking time: 15 mins
Servings: 4
Ingredients:

- 1 head cauliflower, riced (or use store-bought cauliflower rice)
- 2 tbsps olive oil
- 2 pieces garlic, crushed
- 1 teacup cubed carrots
- 1 teacup frozen peas
- 2 eggs, whisked
- 2 tbsps low-sodium soy sauce
- 1 tsp sesame oil
- Green onions for garnish (elective)

Directions:

1. Inside your big griddle or wok, warm olive oil in a med-high temp.

2. Include crushed garlic and sauté for around 1 min till fragrant.

3. Include cubed carrots then cook for 3-4 mins 'til they start to soften.

4. Stir in the cauliflower rice and frozen peas. Cook for an extra 4-5 mins 'til the cauliflower rice is soft and the peas are fully heated.

5. Push your cauliflower solution to the sides of your griddle, creating a well in the center. Pour your whisked eggs into the well and scramble till they are fully cooked.

6. Mix the scrambled eggs into the cauliflower solution.

7. Spray low-sodium soy sauce and sesame oil over the cauliflower fried rice. Stir well to blend.

8. Garnish using severed green onions if anticipated and present.

Per serving: Calories: 160kcal; Fat: 9g; Carbs: 13g; Sugar: 4g; Protein: 7g; Sodium: 320mg; Potassium: 450mg

63. Grilled Tuna Steaks

Degree of difficulty: ★★☆☆

Preparation time: 10 mins

Cooking time: 8 mins

Servings: 4

Ingredients:

- 4 tuna steaks
- 2 tbsps olive oil
- 2 pieces garlic, crushed
- Juice of 1 lemon
- Salt and pepper as required
- Fresh parsley for garnish (elective)

Directions:

1. Warm up your grill to med-high temp.

2. Inside your container, whisk collectively olive oil, crushed garlic, lemon juice, salt, and pepper.

3. Brush the tuna steaks using the olive oil solution.

4. Grill the tuna steaks for around 3-4 mins on all sides for medium-rare (adjust cooking time to your preference).

5. Take out from the grill, garnish with fresh parsley (if anticipated), and present.

Per serving: Calories: 220kcal; Fat: 11g; Carbs: 1g; Sugar: 0g; Protein: 29g; Sodium: 50mg; Potassium: 470mg

64. Lemon Rosemary Grilled Chicken

Degree of difficulty: ★★☆☆

Preparation time: 15 mins

Cooking time: 15 mins

Servings: 4

Ingredients:

- 4 boneless, skinless chicken breasts
- 2 tbsps olive oil
- Juice of 1 lemon
- Zest of 1 lemon
- 2 pieces garlic, crushed
- 1 tbsp fresh rosemary, severed
- Salt and pepper as required
- Fresh rosemary sprigs for garnish (elective)

Directions:

1. Warm up your grill to med-high temp.

2. Inside your container, blend olive oil, lemon juice, lemon zest, crushed garlic, severed rosemary, salt, and pepper.

3. Brush the chicken breasts with the lemon rosemary solution.

4. Grill the chicken for around 6-7 mins on all sides or 'til they are fully cooked and no longer pink in the center.

5. Take out from the grill, garnish with fresh rosemary sprigs (if anticipated), and present.

Per serving: Calories: 240kcal; Fat: 11g; Carbs: 1g; Sugar: 0g; Protein: 32g; Sodium: 100mg; Potassium: 440mg

65. Garlic Herb Roasted Vegetables

Degree of difficulty: ★★☆☆☆

Preparation time: 10 mins

Cooking time: 25 mins

Servings: 4

Ingredients:

- 4 teacups mixed vegetables (e.g., bell peppers, zucchini, cherry tomatoes, broccoli)
- 2 tbsps olive oil
- 3 pieces garlic, crushed
- 1 tsp dried Italian seasoning
- Salt and pepper as required
- Fresh basil for garnish (elective)

Directions:

1. Warm up your oven to 425°F.

2. Inside your big container, shake the mixed vegetables with olive oil, crushed garlic, dried Italian seasoning, salt, and pepper 'til they are well covered.

3. Disperse the vegetables in a single layer on your baking sheet.

4. Roast in your warmed up oven for around 20-25 mins or 'til the vegetables are soft and mildly caramelized, stirring once halfway through.

5. Garnish using fresh basil (if anticipated) and present.

Per serving: Calories: 90kcal; Fat: 7g; Carbs: 7g; Sugar: 3g; Protein: 2g; Sodium: 15mg; Potassium: 290mg

66. Stuffed Tomatoes

Degree of difficulty: ★★☆☆☆

Preparation time: 15 mins

Cooking time: 20 mins

Servings: 4

Ingredients:

- 4 big tomatoes
- 1 teacup cooked quinoa
- 1 teacup cooked lean ground turkey or chicken
- 1/2 teacup severed spinach
- 1/2 teacup cubed bell peppers
- 2 pieces garlic, crushed
- 1 tsp dried Italian seasoning
- Salt and pepper as required
- Grated Parmesan cheese for topping (elective)

Directions:

1. Warm up your oven to 375°F.

2. Cut the tops off your tomatoes then scoop out the seeds and pulp to create hollow shells.

3. Inside your container, blend cooked quinoa, cooked ground turkey or chicken, dried Italian seasoning, severed spinach, cubed bell peppers, crushed garlic, salt, and pepper.

4. Stuff each tomato with the quinoa and turkey/chicken solution.

5. Put your filled tomatoes on your baking sheet, and if anticipated, spray with your grated Parmesan cheese.

6. Bake in to your warmed up oven for around 20 mins, or 'til the tomatoes are soft and the filling is fully heated.

7. Present and relish!

Per serving: Calories: 200kcal; Fat: 4g; Carbs: 21g; Sugar: 5g; Protein: 20g; Sodium: 75mg; Potassium: 780mg

67. Turkey Meatballs with Zoodles

Degree of difficulty: ★★☆☆
Preparation time: 20 mins
Cooking time: 20 mins
Servings: 4
Ingredients:
- 1 lb. lean ground turkey
- 1/2 teacup rolled oats
- 1/4 teacup grated Parmesan cheese
- 1/4 teacup severed fresh parsley
- 1/4 teacup severed onion
- 1 egg
- 2 pieces garlic, crushed
- Salt and pepper as required
- 4 medium zucchinis, spiralized into zoodles
- 2 teacups low-sugar marinara sauce
- Fresh basil for garnish (elective)

Directions:

1. Inside your big container, blend lean ground turkey, rolled oats, grated Parmesan cheese, severed fresh parsley, severed onion, egg, crushed garlic, salt, and pepper. Blend thoroughly.

2. Shape your solution into meatballs, about 1-2 inches in diameter.

3. Warm a griddle in a med-high temp. then include the meatballs. Cook for 10-12 mins, turning occasionally, 'til they are browned on all sides then fully cooked.

4. While your meatballs are cooking, spiralize the zucchinis into zoodles.

5. In your separate saucepan, heat the low-sugar marinara sauce in a middling temp.

6. Once the meatballs are cooked, include them to the sauce and simmer for a couple of mins.

7. Present your turkey meatballs and sauce over the zoodles, garnished with fresh basil if anticipated.

Per serving: Calories: 270kcal; Fat: 10g; Carbs: 20g; Sugar: 8g; Protein: 26g; Sodium: 490mg; Potassium: 1060mg

68. Cilantro Lime Chicken

Degree of difficulty: ★★☆☆
Preparation time: 10 mins
Cooking time: 20 mins
Servings: 4
Ingredients:
- 4 boneless, skinless chicken breasts
- 2 tbsps olive oil
- Juice of 2 limes
- Zest of 1 lime
- 2 pieces garlic, crushed
- 1/4 teacup fresh cilantro, severed
- Salt and pepper as required

Directions:

1. Inside your container, blend olive oil, lime juice, lime zest, crushed garlic, severed cilantro, salt, and pepper.

2. Brush the chicken breasts with the cilantro lime solution.

3. Warm a griddle in a med-high temp. then include the chicken breasts. Cook for around 5-7 mins on all sides or 'til they are fully cooked and no longer pink in the center.

4. Take out from your griddle, garnish using additional cilantro if anticipated, and present.

Per serving: Calories: 230kcal; Fat: 10g; Carbs: 2g; Sugar: 0g; Protein: 33g; Sodium: 80mg; Potassium: 580mg

69. Baked Cod with Veggies

Degree of difficulty: ★★☆☆

Preparation time: 15 mins

Cooking time: 20 mins

Servings: 4

Ingredients:

- 4 cod fillets
- 2 teacups mixed vegetables (e.g., broccoli, bell peppers, carrots)
- 2 tbsps olive oil
- 2 pieces garlic, crushed
- Juice of 1 lemon
- Salt and pepper as required
- Fresh dill for garnish (elective)

Directions:

1. Warm up your oven to 375°F.

2. Inside your container, shake the mixed vegetables with olive oil, crushed garlic, lemon juice, salt, and pepper till they are well covered.

3. Put your cod fillets and mixed vegetables on your baking sheet.

4. Bake in to your warmed up oven for 15-20 mins, or 'til the cod flakes simply with a fork and the vegetables are soft.

5. Garnish using fresh dill (if anticipated) and present.

Per serving: Calories: 190kcal; Fat: 7g; Carbs: 6g; Sugar: 2g; Protein: 24g; Sodium: 80mg;

70. Herb Crusted Pork Tenderloin

Degree of difficulty: ★★★☆☆

Preparation time: 15 mins

Cooking time: 25 mins

Servings: 4

Ingredients:

- 1 pork tenderloin (about 1 lb.)
- 2 tbsps Dijon mustard
- 2 pieces garlic, crushed
- 2 tbsps fresh herbs (e.g., rosemary, thyme, sage), severed
- Salt and pepper as required
- Olive oil for searing

Directions:

1. Warm up your oven to 375°F.

2. Inside your container, blend collectively Dijon mustard, crushed garlic, severed fresh herbs, salt, and pepper.

3. Coat the pork tenderloin with the herb and mustard solution.

4. Warm a griddle in a med-high temp. then include a bit of olive oil. Sear your pork tenderloin on all sides till it's browned.

5. Transfer your seared pork tenderloin to your baking dish and roast in your warmed up oven for around 20-25 mins or 'til it reaches an internal temp. of 145°F.

6. Let your pork rest for a couple of mins prior to slicing.

7. Present and relish!

Per serving: Calories: 220kcal; Fat: 8g; Carbs: 1g; Sugar: 0g; Protein: 34g; Sodium: 270mg; Potassium: 590mg

71. Black Bean Stuffed Peppers

Degree of difficulty: ★★★☆☆

Preparation time: 20 mins

Cooking time: 40 mins

Servings: 4

Ingredients:
- 4 big bell peppers, any color
- 1 teacup cooked brown rice
- 1 tin (15 oz) black beans, that is drained and washed
- 1 teacup corn kernels
- 1 teacup cubed tomatoes (tinned or fresh)
- 1/2 teacup cubed red onion
- 1 tsp chili powder
- Salt and pepper as required
- 1 teacup teared up low-fat cheese (elective)

Directions:

1. Warm up your oven to 375°F.

2. Cut the tops off the bell peppers then take out the seeds and membranes.

3. Inside your big container, blend cooked brown rice, black beans, corn, cubed tomatoes, cubed red onion, chili powder, salt, and pepper.

4. Stuff each bell pepper with the black bean and rice solution.

5. Put your filled peppers in your baking dish. If desired, spray teared up low-fat cheese on top.

6. Cover the baking dish using aluminum foil then bake for around 30-40 mins, or 'til the peppers are soft.

7. Take out the foil then bake for an extra 5-10 mins 'til the cheese is dissolved and bubbly.

8. Present and relish!

Per serving: Calories: 220kcal; Fat: 1g; Carbs: 48g; Sugar: 6g; Protein: 10g; Sodium: 220mg; Potassium: 800mg

72. Lemon Garlic Roasted Chicken

Degree of difficulty: ★★☆☆☆

Preparation time: 15 mins

Cooking time: 45 mins

Servings: 4

Ingredients:
- 4 bone-in, skin-on chicken thighs
- 2 tbsps olive oil
- Juice of 2 lemons
- Zest of 1 lemon
- 4 pieces garlic, crushed
- 1 tbsp fresh rosemary, severed
- Salt and pepper as required

Directions:

1. Warm up your oven to 375°F.

2. Inside your container, whisk collectively olive oil, lemon juice, lemon zest, crushed garlic, severed rosemary, salt, and pepper.

3. Put your chicken thighs in your baking dish then pour the lemon garlic solution over them. Make sure the chicken is well covered.

4. Roast in to your warmed up oven for around 40-45 mins, or 'til the chicken is fully cooked and the skin is crispy.

5. Present and relish!

Per serving: Calories: 350kcal; Fat: 24g; Carbs: 3g; Sugar: 1g; Protein: 30g; Sodium: 140mg; Potassium: 430mg

73. Balsamic Glazed Salmon

Degree of difficulty: ★★☆☆

Preparation time: 10 mins

Cooking time: 15 mins

Servings: 4

Ingredients:

- 4 salmon fillets
- 1/4 teacup balsamic vinegar
- 2 tbsps olive oil
- 2 pieces garlic, crushed
- 2 tbsps honey (elective, for a touch of sweetness)
- Salt and pepper as required
- Fresh basil for garnish (elective)

Directions:

1. Inside your container, whisk collectively balsamic vinegar, olive oil, crushed garlic, honey (if using), salt, and pepper.

2. Put your salmon fillets in a resealable plastic bag then pour the balsamic solution over them. Seal the bag then marinate in your fridge for almost 15 mins.

3. Warm up grill or your grill pan to med-high temp.

4. Grill the salmon for around 3-4 mins on all sides or 'til it's cooked to your desired level of doneness.

5. Take out from the grill, garnish with fresh basil (if anticipated), and present.

Per serving: Calories: 280kcal; Fat: 14g; Carbs: 10g; Sugar: 8g; Protein: 27g; Sodium: 75mg; Potassium: 620mg

74. Shrimp & Veggie Sauté

Degree of difficulty: ★★☆☆

Preparation time: 15 mins

Cooking time: 10 mins

Servings: 4

Ingredients:

- 1 lb. big shrimp, skinned and deveined
- 2 tbsps olive oil
- 2 pieces garlic, crushed
- 1 teacup cherry tomatoes, divided
- 2 teacups broccoli florets
- 1 teacup bell peppers, carved
- Juice of 1 lemon
- Salt and pepper as required
- Fresh parsley for garnish (elective)

Directions:

1. Inside your big griddle, warm olive oil in a med-high temp.

2. Include crushed garlic and sauté for around 1 min till fragrant.

3. Include shrimp to your griddle then cook for around 2-3 mins on all sides or 'til they turn pink and opaque. Take out the shrimp from your griddle then put away.

4. Inside your similar griddle, include cherry tomatoes, broccoli florets, and carved bell peppers. Sauté for around 5-7 mins 'til the vegetables are soft-crisp.

5. Return your cooked shrimp to your griddle, include lemon juice, salt, and pepper. Stir well to blend and heat through.

6. Garnish using fresh parsley (if anticipated) and present.

Per serving: Calories: 180kcal; Fat: 8g; Carbs: 9g; Sugar: 3g; Protein: 18g; Sodium: 230mg; Potassium: 490mg

75. Grilled Eggplant Steaks

Degree of difficulty: ★★☆☆☆

Preparation time: 15 mins

Cooking time: 15 mins

Servings: 4

Ingredients:

- 2 big eggplants, carved into 1/2-inch thick rounds
- 2 tbsps olive oil
- 2 pieces garlic, crushed
- 1 tsp dried oregano
- Salt and pepper as required
- 1/4 teacup severed fresh basil

Directions:

1. Warm up your grill to med-high temp.

2. Inside your container, blend collectively olive oil, crushed garlic, dried oregano, salt, and pepper.

3. Brush both sides of your eggplant slices using the olive oil solution.

4. Grill your eggplant slices for around 3-4 mins on all sides or 'til they are soft and have grill marks.

5. Take out from the grill, garnish with severed fresh basil, and present.

Per serving: Calories: 80kcal; Fat: 4g; Carbs: 11g; Sugar: 5g; Protein: 2g; Sodium: 5mg; Potassium: 370mg

Recipes for Sweets

76. Baked Apple Slices

Degree of difficulty: ★★☆☆☆

Preparation time: 5 mins

Cooking time: 20 mins

Servings: 2

Ingredients:

- 2 apples, finely carved
- 1 tsp cinnamon
- 1/2 tsp nutmeg

Directions:

1. Warm up your oven to 350°F.

2. Inside your container, shake the apple slices with cinnamon and nutmeg.

3. Disperse the apple slices uniformly on your baking sheet.

4. Bake for around 20 mins or 'til the apples are soft and mildly caramelized.

Per serving: Calories: 90kcal; Fat: 0.5g; Carbs: 23g; Sugar: 17g; Protein: 0.5g; Sodium: 0mg; Potassium: 195mg

77. Berry Gelatin

Degree of difficulty: ★☆☆☆☆

Preparation time: 5 mins

Cooking time: 0 mins

Servings: 4

Ingredients:

- 2 teacups mixed berries (e.g., strawberries, blueberries, raspberries)
- 1 packet sugar-free gelatin
- 1 teacup boiling water

Directions:

1. Put your mixed berries inside a container.

2. Dissolve your sugar-free gelatin in 1 teacup of boiling water, stirring till fully dissolved.

3. Pour your gelatin solution over the berries.

4. Stir to blend and put in the fridge till set, usually about 2 hrs.

Per serving: Calories: 20kcal; Fat: 0g; Carbs: 4g; Sugar: 1g; Protein: 1g; Sodium: 20mg; Potassium: 50mg

78. Almond Butter Cookies

Degree of difficulty: ★★★☆☆

Preparation time: 10 mins

Cooking time: 10 mins

Servings: 12

Ingredients:

- 1 teacup almond butter
- 1/4 teacup honey or maple syrup
- 1 egg
- 1/2 tsp baking soda
- 1/2 tsp vanilla extract

Directions:

1. Warm up your oven to 350°F.

2. Inside your blending container, blend almond butter, honey or maple syrup, egg, baking soda, and vanilla extract.

3. Mix till well blended.

4. Drop spoonful of the dough onto your baking sheet covered using parchment paper.

5. Flatten each cookie with a fork.

6. Bake for around 10 mins or 'til the edges are mildly golden.

Per serving: Calories: 150kcal; Fat: 11g; Carbs: 10g; Sugar: 7g; Protein: 5g; Sodium: 65mg; Potassium: 145mg

79. Cocoa-Dusted Almonds

Degree of difficulty: ★☆☆☆☆

Preparation time: 5 mins

Cooking time: 0 mins

Servings: 4

Ingredients:

- 1 teacup raw almonds
- 1 tbsp unsweetened cocoa powder
- 1 tbsp powdered stevia (or sweetener of choice)

Directions:

1. Inside your container, blend the cocoa powder and powdered stevia.

2. Shake the almonds in the cocoa solution till well covered.

Per serving: Calories: 190kcal; Fat: 16g; Carbs: 8g; Sugar: 1g; Protein: 7g; Sodium: 0mg; Potassium: 225mg

80. Frozen Banana Bites

Degree of difficulty: ★★☆☆☆

Preparation time: 10 mins

Cooking time: 0 mins

Servings: 4

Ingredients:

- 2 bananas, skinned and carved into rounds
- 2 tbsps almond butter
- 1/4 teacup unsweetened teared up coconut

Directions:

1. Disperse a thin layer of your almond butter on one side of each banana round.

2. Sandwich two banana rounds together, creating a "bite."

3. Roll the edges in the teared up coconut.

4. Put your banana bites on a tray then freeze for almost 2 hrs prior to presenting.

Per serving: Calories: 110kcal; Fat: 6g; Carbs: 13g; Sugar: 6g; Protein: 2g; Sodium: 0mg; Potassium: 230mg

81. Greek Yogurt Popsicles

Degree of difficulty: ★★☆☆☆

Preparation time: 10 mins

Cooking time: 0 mins

Servings: 4

Ingredients:

- 2 teacups plain Greek yogurt
- 1/4 teacup honey or maple syrup
- 1 tsp vanilla extract
- 1 teacup mixed berries (e.g., blueberries, strawberries)

Directions:

1. Inside your container, mix Greek yogurt, honey or maple syrup, and vanilla extract 'til well blended.

2. Gently wrap in the mixed berries.

3. Pour your solution into popsicle molds.

4. Insert your popsicle sticks then freeze for almost 4 hrs or 'til solid.

Per serving: Calories: 150kcal; Fat: 3g; Carbs: 25g; Sugar: 19g; Protein: 9g; Sodium: 40mg; Potassium: 225mg

82. Dark Chocolate Covered Strawberries

Degree of difficulty: ★★☆☆

Preparation time: 15 mins

Cooking time: 0 mins

Servings: 4

Ingredients:

- 1 teacup dark chocolate chips (that is 70% cocoa or higher)
- 2 teacups fresh strawberries, washed and dried

Directions:

1. Melt your dark chocolate chips in a microwave-safe container in 20-second intervals, stirring in between 'til smooth.

2. Dip each strawberry into your dissolved chocolate, coating about half of each strawberry.

3. Put your chocolate-covered strawberries on a parchment paper-covered tray.

4. Let them cool in the fridge for around 30 mins or 'til the chocolate hardens.

Per serving: Calories: 180kcal; Fat: 11g; Carbs: 22g; Sugar: 12g; Protein: 2g; Sodium: 0mg; Potassium: 195mg

83. Apple Cinnamon Muffins

Degree of difficulty: ★★★☆

Preparation time: 15 mins

Cooking time: 20 mins

Servings: 12

Ingredients:

- 2 teacups almond flour
- 2 tsps baking powder
- 1 tsp ground cinnamon
- 2 medium apples, skinned, cored, and cubed
- 3 big eggs
- 1/4 teacup honey or maple syrup
- 1/4 teacup unsweetened applesauce
- 1 tsp vanilla extract

Directions:

1. Warm up your oven to 350 deg. F then line a muffin tin using paper liners.

2. Inside your container, mix almond flour, baking powder, and ground cinnamon.

3. Inside your extra container, whisk collectively eggs, honey or maple syrup, applesauce, and vanilla extract.

4. Put your wet and dry components, then wrap in the cubed apples.

5. Spoon your batter into the muffin teacups, filling each about 2/3 full.

6. Bake for around 20 mins or 'til a toothpick comes out clean when placed into your muffin.

Per serving: Calories: 160kcal; Fat: 10g; Carbs: 13g; Sugar: 7g; Protein: 5g; Sodium: 20mg; Potassium: 80mg

84. Vanilla Pudding with Berries

Degree of difficulty: ★★☆☆

Preparation time: 10 mins

Cooking time: 0 mins

Servings: 4

Ingredients:

- 2 teacups unsweetened almond milk
- 1/4 teacup cornstarch
- 1/4 teacup honey or maple syrup
- 1 tsp vanilla extract
- 1 teacup mixed berries (e.g., raspberries, blueberries)

Directions:

1. Inside a saucepot, whisk collectively almond milk, cornstarch, honey or maple syrup, and vanilla extract.

2. Cook in a middling temp., mixing regularly till the solution thickens (around 5-7 mins).

3. Take out from temp. then allow it to cool.

4. Once cooled, spoon the pudding into serving dishes, and top with mixed berries.

5. Chill in the fridge for almost 2 hrs prior to presenting.

Per serving: Calories: 120kcal; Fat: 2.5g; Carbs: 25g; Sugar: 17g; Protein: 1g; Sodium: 120mg; Potassium: 45mg

85. Pumpkin Spice Muffins

Degree of difficulty: ★★★☆☆

Preparation time: 15 mins

Cooking time: 25 mins

Servings: 12

Ingredients:

- 2 teacups almond flour
- 2 tsps baking powder
- 1 tsp ground cinnamon
- 1/2 tsp ground nutmeg
- 1/2 tsp ground pieces
- 1/2 tsp ground ginger
- 1 teacup tinned pumpkin puree
- 1/4 teacup honey or maple syrup
- 3 big eggs
- 1/4 teacup unsweetened almond milk

Directions:

1. Warm up your oven to 350 deg. F then line a muffin tin using paper liners.

2. Inside your container, mix almond flour, baking powder, and all the spices.

3. Inside your extra container, whisk collectively pumpkin puree, honey or maple syrup, eggs, and almond milk.

4. Put your wet and dry components, mixing till well blended.

5. Spoon your batter into the muffin teacups, filling each about 2/3 full.

6. Bake for around 25 mins or 'til a toothpick comes out clean when placed into a muffin.

Per serving: Calories: 150kcal; Fat: 9g; Carbs: 13g; Sugar: 7g; Protein: 4g; Sodium: 25mg; Potassium: 90mg

86. Almond Flour Brownies

Degree of difficulty: ★★★☆☆

Preparation time: 10 mins

Cooking time: 25 mins

Servings: 12

Ingredients:

- 2 teacups almond flour
- 1/2 teacup unsweetened cocoa powder
- 1/2 tsp baking soda
- 1/4 tsp salt
- 1/4 teacup honey or maple syrup
- 1/4 teacup dissolved coconut oil
- 2 big eggs
- 1 tsp vanilla extract

Directions:

1. Warm up your oven to 350 deg. F then oil an 8x8-inch baking dish.

2. Inside your container, mix almond flour, cocoa powder, baking soda, and salt.

3. Inside your extra container, whisk collectively honey or maple syrup, dissolved coconut oil, eggs, and vanilla extract.

4. Put your wet and dry components, mixing till well blended.

5. Pour your batter in to your baking dish and disperse it uniformly.

6. Bake for around 25 mins or 'til a toothpick comes out mostly clean when placed into the brownies.

Per serving: Calories: 190kcal; Fat: 15g; Carbs: 12g; Sugar: 5g; Protein: 6g; Sodium: 85mg; Potassium: 40mg

87. Coconut Macaroons

Degree of difficulty: ★★☆☆☆

Preparation time: 10 mins

Cooking time: 15 mins

Servings: 12

Ingredients:

- 2 teacups unsweetened teared up coconut
- 1/4 teacup honey or maple syrup
- 2 big egg whites
- 1/2 tsp vanilla extract
- Tweak of salt

Directions:

1. Warm up your oven to 325 deg. F then line your baking sheet using parchment paper.

2. Inside your container, mix teared up coconut, honey or maple syrup, vanilla extract, then a tweak of salt.

3. Inside your extra container, beat the egg whites 'til stiff peaks form.

4. Gently wrap your whisked egg whites into the coconut solution.

5. Drop spoonful of the solution onto the prepared baking sheet.

6. Bake for around 15 mins or 'til the macaroons turn golden brown.

Per serving: Calories: 90kcal; Fat: 5g; Carbs: 10g; Sugar: 7g; Protein: 1g; Sodium: 20mg; Potassium: 45mg

88. Baked Pears with Cinnamon

Degree of difficulty: ★★☆☆

Preparation time: 10 mins

Cooking time: 30 mins

Servings: 4

Ingredients:

- 4 ripe pears, divided and cored
- 1 tsp cinnamon
- 2 tbsps honey or maple syrup

Directions:

1. Warm up your oven to 375°F.

2. Put your pear halves on your baking sheet.

3. Spray the cinnamon uniformly over the pears and spray with honey or maple syrup.

4. Bake for around 30 mins or 'til the pears are soft.

Per serving: Calories: 120kcal; Fat: 0.5g; Carbs: 31g; Sugar: 19g; Protein: 0.5g; Sodium: 0mg; Potassium: 190mg

89. Cocoa Avocado Mousse

Degree of difficulty: ★★☆☆

Preparation time: 10 mins

Cooking time: 0 mins

Servings: 4

Ingredients:

- 2 ripe avocados, skinned and eroded
- 1/4 teacup unsweetened cocoa powder
- 1/4 teacup honey or maple syrup
- 1/2 tsp vanilla extract

Directions:

1. In blender or your blending container, blend honey or maple syrup, avocados, cocoa powder, and vanilla extract.

2. Blend 'til smooth and creamy.

3. Chill the mousse in the fridge for almost 1 hr prior to presenting.

Per serving: Calories: 210kcal; Fat: 13g; Carbs: 28g; Sugar: 17g; Protein: 2g; Sodium: 0mg; Potassium: 490mg

90. Banana Ice Cream

Degree of difficulty: ★★☆☆

Preparation time: 5 mins

Cooking time: 0 mins

Servings: 4

Ingredients:

- 4 ripe bananas, carved and frozen
- 1/2 tsp vanilla extract
- 1/4 teacup unsweetened almond milk

Directions:

1. Put your frozen banana slices in blender or your blending container.

2. Include vanilla extract and almond milk.

3. Blend till the solution reaches a creamy ice cream consistency.

4. Transfer to a container then freeze for an extra 2 hrs or 'til firm.

Per serving: Calories: 100kcal; Fat: 0.5g; Carbs: 26g; Sugar: 13g; Protein: 1g; Sodium: 0mg; Potassium: 400mg

91. Lemon Poppy Seed Muffins

Degree of difficulty: ★★★☆

Preparation time: 15 mins

Cooking time: 20 mins

Servings: 12

Ingredients:

- 2 teacups almond flour
- 2 tbsps poppy seeds
- 1/2 tsp baking soda
- 1/4 tsp salt
- Zest and juice of 2 lemons
- 1/4 teacup honey or maple syrup
- 3 big eggs
- 1/4 teacup dissolved coconut oil

Directions:

1. Warm up your oven to 350 deg. F then line a muffin tin using paper liners.

2. Inside your container, mix almond flour, poppy seeds, baking soda, and salt.

3. Inside your extra container, whisk collectively lemon zest, lemon juice, honey or maple syrup, eggs, and dissolved coconut oil.

4. Put your wet and dry components, mixing till well blended.

5. Spoon your batter in to your muffin teacups, filling each about 2/3 full.

6. Bake for around 20 mins or 'til a toothpick comes out clean when placed into a muffin.

Per serving: Calories: 160kcal; Fat: 12g; Carbs: 8g; Sugar: 5g; Protein: 5g; Sodium: 85mg; Potassium: 20mg

92. Raspberry Almond Bars

Degree of difficulty: ★★★☆☆

Preparation time: 15 mins

Cooking time: 25 mins

Servings: 12

Ingredients:

- 2 teacups almond flour
- 1/4 teacup honey or maple syrup
- 1/4 teacup dissolved coconut oil
- 1/2 tsp almond extract
- 1/2 teacup fresh raspberries

Directions:

1. Warm up your oven to 350 deg. F then line an 8x8-inch baking dish using parchment paper.

2. Inside your container, mix dissolved coconut oil, almond flour, honey or maple syrup, and almond extract till a dough forms.

3. Press 2/3 of your dough uniformly into the bottom of the prepared baking dish.

4. Scatter fresh raspberries over the dough.

5. Crumble the remaining dough uniformly over the raspberries.

6. Bake for around 25 mins or 'til the bars are mildly golden.

7. Let them cool prior to slicing into bars.

Per serving: Calories: 190kcal; Fat: 14g; Carbs: 11g; Sugar: 6g; Protein: 5g; Sodium: 0mg; Potassium: 35mg

93. Baked Peaches

Degree of difficulty: ★★☆☆☆

Preparation time: 10 mins

Cooking time: 20 mins

Servings: 4

Ingredients:

- 4 ripe peaches, divided and eroded
- 1 tsp ground cinnamon
- 2 tbsps honey or maple syrup

Directions:

1. Warm up your oven to 350°F.

2. Put your peach halves on your baking sheet.

3. Spray the ground cinnamon uniformly over the peaches and spray with honey or maple syrup.

4. Bake for around 20 mins or 'til the peaches are soft.

Per serving: Calories: 80kcal; Fat: 0.5g; Carbs: 20g; Sugar: 18g; Protein: 1g; Sodium: 0mg; Potassium: 220mg

94. Coconut & Almond Clusters

Degree of difficulty: ★★☆☆☆

Preparation time: 10 mins

Cooking time: 0 mins

Servings: 12

Ingredients:

- 1 teacup unsweetened teared up coconut
- 1/2 teacup carved almonds
- 1/4 teacup honey or maple syrup
- 1/4 teacup dissolved coconut oil
- 1/2 tsp vanilla extract

Directions:

1. Inside your container, mix teared up coconut, carved almonds, honey or maple syrup, dissolved coconut oil, and vanilla extract.

2. Drop spoonful of the solution onto a parchment paper-covered tray.

3. Let them cool in the fridge for around 30 mins or 'til they firm up.

Per serving: Calories: 110kcal; Fat: 9g; Carbs: 8g; Sugar: 6g; Protein: 1g; Sodium: 0mg; Potassium: 45mg

95. Chocolate Dipped Orange Slices

Degree of difficulty: ★★☆☆☆

Preparation time: 15 mins

Cooking time: 0 mins

Servings: 4

Ingredients:

- 2 oranges, skinned and carved into rounds
- 1/4 teacup dark chocolate chips (that is 70% cocoa or higher)

Directions:

1. Put your orange slices on a parchment paper-covered tray.

2. Melt your dark chocolate chips in your microwave-safe container in 20-second intervals, stirring in between 'til smooth.

3. Dip each orange slice halfway into the dissolved chocolate.

4. Put your chocolate-dipped orange slices back on the tray.

5. Let them cool in the fridge for around 30 mins or 'til the chocolate hardens.

Per serving: Calories: 90kcal; Fat: 3g; Carbs: 17g; Sugar: 13g; Protein: 1g; Sodium: 0mg; Potassium: 210mg

96. Baked Oatmeal with Berries

Degree of difficulty: ★★☆☆

Preparation time: 10 mins

Cooking time: 30 mins

Servings: 4

Ingredients:

- 2 teacups old-fashioned oats
- 1 tsp baking powder
- 1/2 tsp ground cinnamon
- 1/4 tsp salt
- 2 teacups unsweetened almond milk
- 1/4 teacup honey or maple syrup
- 1 tsp vanilla extract
- 1 teacup mixed berries (e.g., blueberries, raspberries)

Directions:

1. Warm up your oven to 350 deg. F then oil an 8x8-inch baking dish.

2. Inside your container, mix oats, baking powder, ground cinnamon, and salt.

3. Inside your extra container, whisk collectively almond milk, honey or maple syrup, and vanilla extract.

4. Put your wet and dry components, mixing till well blended.

5. Gently wrap in the mixed berries.

6. Pour your solution in to your baking dish and disperse it uniformly.

7. Bake for around 30 mins or 'til the oatmeal is set then mildly golden.

Per serving: Calories: 270kcal; Fat: 4.5g; Carbs: 52g; Sugar: 20g; Protein: 6g; Sodium: 200mg; Potassium: 215mg

97. Pineapple Mint Sorbet

Degree of difficulty: ★★☆☆

Preparation time: 10 mins

Cooking time: 0 mins

Servings: 4

Ingredients:

- 2 teacups frozen pineapple chunks
- 1/4 teacup fresh mint leaves
- 1/4 teacup honey or maple syrup
- 1/4 teacup unsweetened coconut milk

Directions:

1. Put your frozen pineapple chunks, fresh mint leaves, honey or maple syrup, and unsweetened coconut milk inside a mixer.

2. Blend 'til smooth and creamy.

3. Transfer your solution to a container then freeze for almost 2 hrs or 'til firm.

4. Present scoops of sorbet with a sprig of fresh mint.

Per serving: Calories: 120kcal; Fat: 0.5g; Carbs: 31g; Sugar: 25g; Protein: 1g; Sodium: 0mg; Potassium: 155mg

98. Baked Cinnamon Apples

Degree of difficulty: ★★☆☆☆

Preparation time: 10 mins

Cooking time: 30 mins

Servings: 4

Ingredients:

- 4 apples, cored and carved
- 1 tsp ground cinnamon
- 2 tbsps honey or maple syrup

Directions:

1. Warm up your oven to 350°F.

2. Inside your container, shake the apple slices with ground cinnamon and honey or maple syrup.

3. Disperse the apple slices uniformly in your baking dish.

4. Bake for around 30 mins or 'til the apples are soft and caramelized.

Per serving: Calories: 100kcal; Fat: 0g; Carbs: 27g; Sugar: 21g; Protein: 0g; Sodium: 0mg; Potassium: 190mg

99. Chocolate Protein Balls

Degree of difficulty: ★★☆☆☆

Preparation time: 15 mins

Cooking time: 0 mins

Servings: 12

Ingredients:

- 1 teacup almond flour
- 1/4 teacup unsweetened cocoa powder
- 1/4 teacup honey or maple syrup
- 1/4 teacup almond butter
- 1 scoop chocolate protein powder (without added sugar)
- 1 tsp vanilla extract

Directions:

1. Inside your container, mix almond flour, cocoa powder, honey or maple syrup, almond butter, chocolate protein powder, and vanilla extract till well blended.

2. Form the solution into 12 small balls.

3. Put your balls on a tray covered using parchment paper then chill in your fridge for around 30 mins or 'til firm.

Per serving: Calories: 110kcal; Fat: 7g; Carbs: 9g; Sugar: 5g; Protein: 4g; Sodium: 0mg; Potassium: 100mg

100. Chocolate-Dipped Banana Slices

Degree of difficulty: ★★☆☆

Preparation time: 15 mins

Cooking time: 0 mins

Servings: 4

Ingredients:

- 2 bananas, skinned and carved into rounds
- 1/4 teacup dark chocolate chips (that is 70% cocoa or higher)

Directions:

1. Put your banana slices on a parchment paper-covered tray.

2. Melt your dark chocolate chips in a microwave-safe container in 20-second intervals, stirring in between 'til smooth.

3. Dip each banana slice halfway into the dissolved chocolate.

4. Put your chocolate-dipped banana slices back on the tray.

5. Let them cool in the fridge for around 30 mins or 'til the chocolate hardens.

Per serving: Calories: 90kcal; Fat: 3g; Carbs: 17g; Sugar: 12g; Protein: 1g; Sodium: 0mg; Potassium: 230mg

Recipes for Snacks

101. Veggie Sticks with Hummus

Degree of difficulty: ★☆☆☆

Preparation time: 10 mins

Cooking time: 0 mins

Servings: 2

Ingredients:

- 2 teacups of mixed vegetable sticks (carrots, cucumbers, bell peppers)
- 1/2 teacup of hummus (low sodium)

Directions:

1. Wash and cut the vegetables into sticks.

2. Present the veggie sticks with hummus as a dip.

Per serving: Calories: 150kcal; Fat: 6g; Carbs: 20g; Sugar: 4g; Protein: 6g; Sodium: 100mg; Potassium: 400mg

102. Roasted Chickpeas

Degree of difficulty: ★★☆☆

Preparation time: 5 mins

Cooking time: 25 mins

Servings: 4

Ingredients:

- 2 tins (15 oz each) of chickpeas (garbanzo beans), that is drained and washed
- 2 tbsps olive oil
- 1 tsp paprika
- 1/2 tsp garlic powder
- Salt and pepper as required

Directions:

1. Warm up your oven to 400°F.

2. Pat your chickpeas dry using a paper towel.

3. Inside your container, shake the chickpeas with olive oil, paprika, garlic powder, salt, and pepper.

4. Disperse your chickpeas on your baking sheet and roast for around 25 mins 'til they become crispy.

Per serving: Calories: 200kcal; Fat: 7g; Carbs: 26g; Sugar: 0g; Protein: 8g; Sodium: 160mg; Potassium: 250mg

103. Greek Yogurt with Nuts

Degree of difficulty: ★☆☆☆☆

Preparation time: 2 mins

Cooking time: 0 mins

Servings: 1

Ingredients:

- 1 teacup of Greek yogurt (low-fat)
- 1 tbsp of severed nuts (e.g., almonds, walnuts)

Directions:

1. Spoon Greek yogurt into a container.

2. Spray severed nuts on top.

Per serving: Calories: 200kcal; Fat: 8g; Carbs: 10g; Sugar: 8g; Protein: 20g; Sodium: 50mg; Potassium: 200mg

104. Apple Slices with Almond Butter

Degree of difficulty: ★☆☆☆☆

Preparation time: 5 mins

Cooking time: 0 mins

Servings: 2

Ingredients:

- 2 medium apples, carved
- 4 tbsps of almond butter (no added sugar)

Directions:

1. Slice the apples.

2. Present the apple slices with almond butter for dipping.

Per serving: Calories: 250kcal; Fat: 15g; Carbs: 30g; Sugar: 20g; Protein: 5g; Sodium: 0mg; Potassium: 260mg

105. Hard-Boiled Eggs

Degree of difficulty: ★★☆☆☆

Preparation time: 2 mins

Cooking time: 10 mins

Servings: 2

Ingredients:

- 4 big eggs

Directions:

1. Put your eggs in a saucepan then cover them with water.

2. Boil water, then decrease the temp. then simmer for 10 mins.

3. Take out from temp., cool the eggs under cold running water, and peel prior to presenting.

Per serving: Calories: 140kcal; Fat: 10g; Carbs: 1g; Sugar: 0g; Protein: 12g; Sodium: 70mg; Potassium: 130mg

106. Spiced Pumpkin Seeds

Degree of difficulty: ★★☆☆☆

Preparation time: 5 mins

Cooking time: 15 mins

Servings: 4

Ingredients:

- 2 teacups raw pumpkin seeds (pepitas)
- 1 tbsp olive oil
- 1 tsp ground cumin
- 1/2 tsp paprika
- 1/2 tsp garlic powder
- Salt as required

Directions:

1. Warm up your oven to 325°F.

2. Inside your container, shake pumpkin seeds with olive oil, cumin, paprika, garlic powder, and a tweak of salt.

3. Disperse the seasoned seeds on your baking sheet then bake for around 15 mins or 'til they become crispy, mixing irregularly.

Per serving: Calories: 200kcal; Fat: 16g; Carbs: 5g; Sugar: 0g; Protein: 10g; Sodium: 200mg; Potassium: 280mg

107. Cheese and Almond Plate

Degree of difficulty: ★☆☆☆☆

Preparation time: 5 mins

Cooking time: 0 mins

Servings: 2

Ingredients:

- 2 oz. of low-fat cheese (e.g., mozzarella, cheddar)
- 1/4 teacup of almonds (unsalted)

Directions:

1. Organize cheese slices on a plate.

2. Present with almonds on the side.

Per serving: Calories: 200kcal; Fat: 14g; Carbs: 4g; Sugar: 1g; Protein: 12g; Sodium: 220mg; Potassium: 180mg

108. Baked Kale Chips

Degree of difficulty: ★★☆☆☆

Preparation time: 10 mins

Cooking time: 15 mins

Servings: 2

Ingredients:

- 4 teacups kale leaves, washed, dried, and torn into bite-sized pieces
- 1 tbsp olive oil
- Salt and pepper as required

Directions:

1. Warm up your oven to 350°F.

2. Inside your container, shake kale pieces with olive oil, salt, and pepper.

3. Disperse the kale on your baking sheet then bake for around 15 mins, or 'til crispy.

Per serving: Calories: 100kcal; Fat: 7g; Carbs: 9g; Sugar: 1g; Protein: 5g; Sodium: 50mg; Potassium: 420mg

109. Cottage Cheese with Sliced Cucumber

Degree of difficulty: ★☆☆☆

Preparation time: 5 mins

Cooking time: 0 mins

Servings: 2

Ingredients:

- 1 teacup low-fat cottage cheese
- 1 small cucumber, finely carved

Directions:

1. Spoon cottage cheese into containers.

2. Top with carved cucumber.

Per serving: Calories: 150kcal; Fat: 2g; Carbs: 10g; Sugar: 5g; Protein: 22g; Sodium: 400mg; Potassium: 280mg

110. Mixed Nuts

Degree of difficulty: ★☆☆☆

Preparation time: 2 mins

Cooking time: 0 mins

Servings: 2

Ingredients:

- 1/2 teacup mixed nuts (e.g., almonds, walnuts, cashews) (unsalted)

Directions:

1. Simply measure out the mixed nuts and relish.

Per serving: Calories: 350kcal; Fat: 30g; Carbs: 10g; Sugar: 2g; Protein: 10g; Sodium: 0mg; Potassium: 380mg

111. Tuna Salad on Celery Sticks

Degree of difficulty: ★★☆☆☆

Preparation time: 10 mins

Cooking time: 0 mins

Servings: 2

Ingredients:

- 1 tin (5 oz) of tinned tuna in water, drained
- 2 tbsps low-fat Greek yogurt
- 1 tsp Dijon mustard
- Salt and pepper as required
- 4 celery stalks, cleaned and cut into sticks

Directions:

1. Inside your container, blend the drained tuna, Greek yogurt, Dijon mustard, salt, and pepper. Blend thoroughly.

2. Spoon the tuna salad onto celery sticks.

Per serving: Calories: 120kcal; Fat: 2g; Carbs: 4g; Sugar: 2g; Protein: 20g; Sodium: 250mg; Potassium: 260mg

112. Cherry Tomatoes with Mozzarella

Degree of difficulty: ★☆☆☆☆

Preparation time: 5 mins

Cooking time: 0 mins

Servings: 2

Ingredients:

- 1 teacup cherry tomatoes
- 2 oz. low-fat mozzarella cheese, cut into small cubes
- Fresh basil leaves (elective)
- Balsamic vinegar (elective)

Directions:

1. Place cherry tomatoes and mozzarella cubes on a plate.

2. Garnish using fresh basil leaves and spray using a small amount of balsamic vinegar if anticipated.

Per serving: Calories: 150kcal; Fat: 8g; Carbs: 5g; Sugar: 3g; Protein: 10g; Sodium: 150mg; Potassium: 250mg

113. Whole Grain Rice Cakes with Avocado

Degree of difficulty: ★☆☆☆☆

Preparation time: 5 mins

Cooking time: 0 mins

Servings: 2

Ingredients:

- 2 whole grain rice cakes
- 1/2 avocado, finely carved
- Tweak of salt and pepper
- Red pepper flakes (elective)

Directions:

1. Place rice cakes on a plate.

2. Top each rice cake with avocado slices.

3. Flavour using a tweak of salt, pepper, and red pepper flakes if anticipated.

Per serving: Calories: 150kcal; Fat: 9g; Carbs: 15g; Sugar: 1g; Protein: 3g; Sodium: 80mg; Potassium: 360mg

114. Roasted Seaweed Sheets

Degree of difficulty: ★☆☆☆☆

Preparation time: 2 mins

Cooking time: 0 mins

Servings: 2

Ingredients:

- 4 sheets of roasted seaweed (nori)

Directions:

1. Simply relish the roasted seaweed sheets as a snack.

Per serving: Calories: 20kcal; Fat: 1g; Carbs: 1g; Sugar: 0g; Protein: 1g; Sodium: 60mg; Potassium: 40mg

115. Cheese and Turkey Roll Ups

Degree of difficulty: ★★☆☆

Preparation time: 5 mins

Cooking time: 0 mins

Servings: 2

Ingredients:

- 4 slices of low-fat turkey breast
- 2 slices of low-fat cheese
- 1/2 cucumber, cut into thin strips

Directions:

1. Lay turkey slices flat.

2. Place a slice of cheese and cucumber strips on each turkey slice.

3. Roll up the turkey slices and secure with toothpicks if needed.

Per serving: Calories: 150kcal; Fat: 5g; Carbs: 4g; Sugar: 2g; Protein: 22g; Sodium: 400mg; Potassium: 200mg

116. Whole Wheat Pita with Tzatziki

Degree of difficulty: ★★☆☆

Preparation time: 5 mins

Cooking time: 0 mins

Servings: 2

Ingredients:

- 2 whole wheat pita bread rounds
- 1/2 teacup tzatziki sauce (low-fat)

Directions:

1. Cut the whole wheat pita bread into wedges.

2. Present with tzatziki sauce for dipping.

Per serving: Calories: 150kcal; Fat: 2g; Carbs: 30g; Sugar: 2g; Protein: 6g; Sodium: 250mg; Potassium: 180mg

117. Edamame with Sea Salt

Degree of difficulty: ★☆☆☆☆

Preparation time: 5 mins

Cooking time: 5 mins

Servings: 2

Ingredients:

- 2 teacups frozen edamame (unshelled)
- Sea salt, as required

Directions:

1. Cook your edamame using the package guidelines.

2. Spray with sea salt prior to presenting.

Per serving: Calories: 120kcal; Fat: 4g; Carbs: 10g; Sugar: 3g; Protein: 10g; Sodium: 5mg; Potassium: 200mg

118. Whole Grain Crackers with Cottage Cheese

Degree of difficulty: ★☆☆☆☆

Preparation time: 2 mins

Cooking time: 0 mins

Servings: 2

Ingredients:

- 8 whole grain crackers
- 1/2 teacup low-fat cottage cheese

Directions:

1. Disperse cottage cheese on the whole grain crackers.

Per serving: Calories: 150kcal; Fat: 4g; Carbs: 20g; Sugar: 2g; Protein: 8g; Sodium: 220mg; Potassium: 120mg

119. Stuffed Mini Bell Peppers

Degree of difficulty: ★★☆☆

Preparation time: 10 mins

Cooking time: 15 mins

Servings: 2

Ingredients:

- 8 mini bell peppers
- 1/2 teacup low-fat cream cheese
- Chopped fresh herbs (e.g., chives, parsley) for garnish (elective)

Directions:

1. Warm up your oven to 375°F.

2. Slice off the tops of the mini bell peppers then take out the seeds.

3. Fill each pepper with a spoonful of low-fat cream cheese.

4. Put your filled peppers on your baking sheet then bake for around 15 mins or 'til peppers are soft.

5. Garnish using severed fresh herbs if anticipated.

Per serving: Calories: 150kcal; Fat: 6g; Carbs: 16g; Sugar: 7g; Protein: 6g; Sodium: 150mg; Potassium: 400mg

120. Baked Sweet Potato Fries

Degree of difficulty: ★★☆☆

Preparation time: 10 mins

Cooking time: 25 mins

Servings: 2

Ingredients:

- 2 medium sweet potatoes, cut into fries
- 1 tbsp olive oil
- Salt and pepper as required

Directions:

1. Warm up your oven to 425°F.

2. Inside your container, shake sweet potato fries with olive oil, salt, and pepper.

3. Disperse the fries on your baking sheet then bake for around 25 mins, turning them once halfway through, till they are crispy.

Per serving: Calories: 150kcal; Fat: 6g; Carbs: 24g; Sugar: 6g; Protein: 2g; Sodium: 150mg; Potassium: 430mg

121. Celery Sticks with Cream Cheese

Degree of difficulty: ★☆☆☆

Preparation time: 5 mins

Cooking time: 0 mins

Servings: 2

Ingredients:

- 4 celery stalks, cleaned and cut into sticks
- 4 tbsps low-fat cream cheese

Directions:

1. Disperse cream cheese onto celery sticks.

Per serving: Calories: 80kcal; Fat: 5g; Carbs: 6g; Sugar: 2g; Protein: 2g; Sodium: 100mg; Potassium: 300mg

122. Cucumber and Tomato Salad

Degree of difficulty: ★☆☆☆

Preparation time: 10 mins

Cooking time: 0 mins

Servings: 2

Ingredients:

- 1 cucumber, carved
- 1 teacup cherry tomatoes, divided
- 2 tbsps balsamic vinegar (low-sodium)
- Fresh basil leaves (elective)
- Salt and pepper as required

Directions:

1. Inside your container, blend cucumber slices and cherry tomato halves.

2. Spray with balsamic vinegar, then flavour using salt and pepper.

3. Garnish using fresh basil leaves if anticipated.

Per serving: Calories: 50kcal; Fat: 0g; Carbs: 12g; Sugar: 7g; Protein: 2g; Sodium: 20mg; Potassium: 350mg

123. Trail Mix with Nuts and Seeds

Degree of difficulty: ★☆☆☆

Preparation time: 2 mins

Cooking time: 0 mins

Servings: 2

Ingredients:

- 1/2 teacup mixed nuts (e.g., almonds, walnuts, cashews)
- 2 tbsps pumpkin seeds (pepitas)
- 2 tbsps sunflower seeds
- 2 tbsps dried cranberries (unsweetened)

Directions:

1. Mix all the components inside a container.

Per serving: Calories: 250kcal; Fat: 18g; Carbs: 17g; Sugar: 8g; Protein: 7g; Sodium: 5mg; Potassium: 280mg

124. Apple and Cheese Slices

Degree of difficulty: ★☆☆☆

Preparation time: 5 mins

Cooking time: 0 mins

Servings: 2

Ingredients:

- 1 apple, finely carved
- 2 slices low-fat cheese (e.g., mozzarella, cheddar)

Directions:

1. Organize apple slices and cheese slices on a plate.

Per serving: Calories: 150kcal; Fat: 6g; Carbs: 20g; Sugar: 15g; Protein: 6g; Sodium: 200mg; Potassium: 180mg

125. Greek Yogurt with Berries and Honey

Degree of difficulty: ★☆☆☆

Preparation time: 5 mins

Cooking time: 0 mins

Servings: 2

Ingredients:

- 1 teacup low-fat Greek yogurt
- 1/2 teacup mixed berries (e.g., strawberries, blueberries, raspberries)
- 2 tsps honey (elective)

Directions:

1. Spoon Greek yogurt into containers.

2. Top using mixed berries then spray using honey if anticipated.

Per serving: Calories: 160kcal; Fat: 1g; Carbs: 30g; Sugar: 25g; Protein: 10g; Sodium: 60mg; Potassium: 230mg

Fitness Guide

Physical exercise is a cornerstone of the GOLO diet plan, working in tandem with dietary adjustments and the use of the Release supplement to achieve weight loss and improved insulin management.

The Synergy Between Exercise and the GOLO Diet

The GOLO diet is built on the premise that achieving weight loss and improved insulin management is a holistic endeavor. While dietary choices and the use of the Release supplement are central components, physical exercise completes the equation. Here's how exercise and the GOLO diet work in tandem:

1. **Enhanced Calorie Expenditure:** Exercise increases the number of calories your body burns, creating a calorie deficit when blended with dietary changes. This deficit is crucial for weight loss because it helps the body tap into its fat stores for energy, resulting in a reduction in overall body weight.

2. **Improved Insulin Sensitivity:** Regular physical activity enhances insulin sensitivity, making your body's cells more responsive to insulin's signals. As insulin sensitivity improves, blood sugar levels stabilize, reducing the risk of insulin resistance and associated health problems.

3. **Appetite Regulation:** Exercise can help regulate appetite hormones, reducing feelings of hunger and preventing overeating. This is especially important in maintaining a calorie deficit for weight loss.

4. **Metabolic Boost:** Physical activity revs up your metabolism, increasing the rate at which your body burns calories even when at rest. This metabolic boost contributes to sustainable weight loss.

Benefits of Physical Exercise in the GOLO Diet

Let's explore the specific benefits of incorporating regular physical exercise into your GOLO diet plan:

1. **Weight Loss:** Exercise is a powerful tool for shedding extra lbs.. It helps create a calorie deficit by burning calories and stimulates the breakdown of stored fat for energy. Over time, consistent exercise can lead to significant weight loss when blended with a balanced diet.

2. **Insulin Sensitivity:** Physical activity enhances the body's ability to use insulin effectively. This means that glucose is transported into cells more efficiently, leading to better blood sugar control and a reduced risk of insulin resistance, prediabetes, and type 2 diabetes.

3. **Muscle Preservation:** When you lose weight, you want to prioritize the loss of fat while preserving lean muscle mass. Regular exercise, particularly resistance training (weightlifting), helps maintain muscle, contributing to a healthier body composition.

4. **Blood Sugar Regulation:** Exercise can lead to immediate improvements in blood sugar levels. Even a single bout of moderate-intensity exercise can enhance insulin sensitivity and lower blood sugar levels.

5. **Cardiovascular Health:** Engaging in physical activity has a beneficial effect on heart health by decreasing the likelihood of cardiovascular conditions like hypertension, elevated cholesterol levels, and coronary artery disease. It fortifies the heart and enhances blood circulation.

6. **Mood and Mental Health:** Exercise releases endorphins, which are natural mood enhancers. Exercise can alleviate stress, anxiety, and depression, all of which can contribute to an enhanced overall sense of well-being.

7. **Energy and Vitality:** Regular exercise can increase your energy levels and enhance your vitality, making it easier to stay active & maintain a healthy lifestyle.

8. **Improved Sleep:** Quality sleep is essential for weight management and insulin sensitivity. Exercise can promote better sleep patterns, helping you get the rest you need.

Incorporating Exercise into Your GOLO Diet Plan

To maximize the benefits of physical exercise in the context of the GOLO diet, consider the following tips:

1. **Choose Activities You Enjoy:** Whether it's walking, jogging, swimming, cycling, dancing, or any other form of exercise, pick activities that you find enjoyable. This will increase your motivation to stick with a regular exercise routine.

2. **Start Slowly:** If you are new to exercise or have been leading a sedentary lifestyle for an extended period, it's advisable to commence with low-impact activities and progressively ramp up the intensity and duration as you go along. Consult with a healthcare professional if you have any health concerns or medical conditions.

3. **Mix Cardio & Strength Training:** Combining cardiovascular exercises (e.g., jogging, cycling) with strength training (e.g., weightlifting, bodyweight exercises) offers a comprehensive approach to fitness. Cardio burns calories, while strength training builds muscle and boosts metabolism.

4. **Set Realistic Goals:** Establish achievable fitness goals that align with your GOLO diet objectives. Whether it's a specific weight loss target, improved endurance, or increased strength, setting realistic goals can help keep you motivated.

5. **Prioritize Consistency:** Consistency is key to reaping the benefits of exercise. Aim for regular, consistent workouts, even if they are shorter in duration. It's better to exercise consistently over time than to sporadically engage in long, intense sessions.

6. **Mix It Up:** Variety in your exercise routine can prevent boredom and plateaus. Consider trying different types of workouts to keep things interesting.

7. **Warm Up and Cool Down:** Always start your exercise session with a warm-up to prepare your muscles and joints and end with a cool-down to reduce the risk of injury and muscle soreness.

8. **Listen to Your Body:** Pay attention to how your body responds to exercise. If you experience pain or discomfort, consult with a healthcare professional. It's essential to exercise safely.

Sample Exercise Routine for the GOLO Diet

Here's a sample exercise routine that you can incorporate into your GOLO diet plan:

Day 1: Cardiovascular Exercise

- 30 mins of brisk walking or cycling

Day 2: Strength Training

- Bodyweight exercises (push-ups, squats, lunges) - 3 sets of 12-15 reps
- Planks - 3 sets of 30-60 seconds

Day 3: Active Rest

- Yoga or stretching routine for flexibility and relaxation

Day 4: Cardiovascular Exercise

- 30 mins of jogging or swimming

Day 5: Strength Training

- Dumbbell or resistance band exercises (bicep curls, tricep extensions, overhead press) - 3 sets of 12-15 reps
- Leg lifts or glute bridges - 3 sets of 12-15 reps

Day 6: Cardiovascular Exercise

- 30 mins of high-intensity interval training (HIIT) or circuit training

Day 7: Rest

- Allow your body to recover

This routine provides a balance of cardio and strength training, promoting weight loss and muscle maintenance. Modify the intensity and duration according to your fitness level and personal preferences.

Conversion Chart

Volume Equivalents (Liquid)

US Standard	US Standard (oz.)	Metric (approximate)
2 tbsps.	1 fl. oz.	30 milliliter
¼ cup	2 fl. oz.	60 milliliter
½ cup	4 fl. oz.	120 milliliter
1 cup	8 fl. oz.	240 milliliter
1½ cups	12 fl. oz.	355 milliliter
2 cups or 1 pint	16 fl. oz.	475 milliliter
4 cups or 1 quart	32 fl. oz.	1 Liter
1 gallon	128 fl. oz.	4 Liter

Volume Equivalents (Dry)

US Standard	Metric (approximate)
⅛ tsp.	0.5 milliliter
¼ tsp.	1 milliliter
½ tsp.	2 milliliter
¾ tsp.	4 milliliter
1 tsp.	5 milliliter
1 tbsp.	15 milliliter
¼ cup	59 milliliter
⅓ cup	79 milliliter
½ cup	118 milliliter
⅔ cup	156 milliliter
¾ cup	177 milliliter
1 cup	235 milliliter
2 cups or 1 pint	475 milliliter

3 cups	700 milliliter
4 cups or 1 quart	1 Liter

Oven Temperatures

Fahrenheit (F)	Celsius (C) (approximate)
250 deg.F	120 deg.C
300 deg.F	150 deg.C
325 deg.F	165 deg.C
350 deg.F	180 deg.C
375 deg.F	190 deg.C
400 deg.F	200 deg.C
425 deg.F	220 deg.C
450 deg.F	230 deg.C

Weight Equivalents

US Standard	Metric (approximate)
1 tbsp.	15 g
½ oz.	15 g
1 oz.	30 g
2 oz.	60 g
4 oz.	115 g
8 oz.	225 g
12 oz.	340 g
16 oz. or 1 lbs.	455 g

70 Days Meal Plan

Day	Breakfast	Lunch	Dinner	Dessert
1	Banana Nut Muffins	Turkey Club Lettuce Wrap	Balsamic Glazed Chicken	Dark Chocolate Covered Strawberries
2	Quinoa Breakfast Bowl	Grilled Chicken Salad	Shrimp & Veggie Sautè	Almond Flour Brownies
3	Avocado Egg Salad	Chickpea Salad	Grilled Tuna Steaks	Raspberry Almond Bars
4	Tofu Scramble with Veggies	Avocado & Tuna Salad	Stuffed Acorn Squash	Baked Cinnamon Apples
5	Spinach and Mushroom Scramble	Tomato Basil Soup	Garlic Herb Roasted Vegetables	Chocolate Protein Balls
6	Vegetable Frittata	Egg Salad Lettuce Wraps	Tofu Stir Fry	Chocolate-Dipped Banana Slices
7	Blueberry Protein Pancakes	Bean and Veggie Soup	Stuffed Tomatoes	Cocoa-Dusted Almonds
8	Whole Wheat Blueberry Pancakes	Balsamic Veggie Bowl	Baked Lemon Herb Chicken	Apple Cinnamon Muffins
9	Mushroom and Tomato Breakfast Skillet	Turkey & Veggie Skillet	Grilled Steak with Veggies	Greek Yogurt Popsicles
10	Spinach and Feta Wrap	Spinach & Quinoa Stuffed Peppers	Baked Cod with Veggies	Coconut Macaroons
11	Cottage Cheese with Pineapple	Caprese Salad	Garlic Shrimp Zoodle	Baked Oatmeal with Berries
12	Zucchini Breakfast Muffins	Tomato & Cucumber Salad	Chicken Fajita Bowl	Vanilla Pudding with Berries

13	Sausage & Veggie Breakfast Skillet	Grilled Chicken & Veggie Skewers	Grilled Salmon with Asparagus	Lemon Poppy Seed Muffins
14	Breakfast Tacos with Salsa	Avocado & Tuna Salad	Herb Crusted Pork Tenderloin	Cocoa Avocado Mousse
15	Cottage Cheese and Peach Bowl	Lentil Soup	Lemon Rosemary Grilled Chicken	Pineapple Mint Sorbet
16	Almond and Berry Granola	Grilled Portobello Mushrooms	Black Bean Stuffed Peppers	Baked Peaches
17	Fruit Salad with Cinnamon	Spinach & Feta Stuffed Chicken	Cauliflower Fried Rice	Coconut & Almond Clusters
18	Berry Smoothie	Shrimp & Veggie Stir Fry	Lemon Butter Tilapia	Chocolate Dipped Orange Slices
19	Almond Butter Toast	Baked Eggs with Spinach	Balsamic Glazed Chicken	Baked Apple Slices
20	Overnight Oats with Berries	Cilantro Lime Chicken	Grilled Tuna Steaks	Banana Ice Cream
21	Turkey and Avocado Wrap	Pesto Chicken Salad	Balsamic Glazed Salmon	Greek Yogurt Popsicles
22	Buckwheat Pancakes	Baked Cod with Veggies	Garlic Herb Roasted Vegetables	Dark Chocolate Covered Strawberries
23	Vegetable Frittata	Chickpea Salad	Tofu Stir Fry	Apple Cinnamon Muffins
24	Turkey and Avocado Wrap	Spinach & Berry Salad	Stuffed Acorn Squash	Cocoa-Dusted Almonds

25	Avocado Egg Salad	Tomato Basil Soup	Grilled Lemon Herb Chicken	Baked Oatmeal with Berries
26	Cottage Cheese with Pineapple	Egg Salad Lettuce Wraps	Turkey Meatballs With Zoodles	Vanilla Pudding with Berries
27	Blueberry Protein Pancakes	Grilled Portobello Mushrooms	Lemon Garlic Roasted Chicken	Coconut Macaroons
28	Whole Wheat Blueberry Pancakes	Balsamic Veggie Bowl	Garlic Shrimp Zoodle	Baked Peaches
29	Mushroom and Tomato Breakfast Skillet	Turkey Club Lettuce Wrap	Grilled Steak with Veggies	Cocoa Avocado Mousse
30	Spinach and Feta Wrap	Spinach & Quinoa Stuffed Peppers	Spaghetti Squash Primavera	Pineapple Mint Sorbet
31	Banana Nut Muffins	Grilled Chicken Salad	Grilled Tuna Steaks	Baked Cinnamon Apples
32	Quinoa Breakfast Bowl	Chickpea Salad	Stuffed Acorn Squash	Chocolate Protein Balls
33	Avocado Egg Salad	Spinach & Berry Salad	Garlic Herb Roasted Vegetables	Chocolate-Dipped Banana Slices
34	Tofu Scramble with Veggies	Spinach & Feta Stuffed Chicken	Tofu Stir Fry	Cocoa-Dusted Almonds
35	Spinach and Mushroom Scramble	Pesto Chicken Salad	Stuffed Tomatoes	Apple Cinnamon Muffins
36	Vegetable Frittata	Bean and Veggie Soup	Baked Lemon Herb Chicken	Greek Yogurt Popsicles

37	Blueberry Protein Pancakes	Cilantro Lime Chicken	Grilled Steak with Veggies	Coconut Macaroons
38	Whole Wheat Blueberry Pancakes	Turkey & Veggie Skillet	Baked Cod with Veggies	Baked Oatmeal with Berries
39	Mushroom and Tomato Breakfast Skillet	Spinach & Quinoa Stuffed Peppers	Garlic Shrimp Zoodle	Vanilla Pudding with Berries
40	Spinach and Feta Wrap	Caprese Salad	Chicken Fajita Bowl	Lemon Poppy Seed Muffins
41	Cottage Cheese with Pineapple	Tomato & Cucumber Salad	Grilled Salmon with Asparagus	Cocoa Avocado Mousse
42	Zucchini Breakfast Muffins	Grilled Chicken & Veggie Skewers	Herb Crusted Pork Tenderloin	Pineapple Mint Sorbet
43	Sausage & Veggie Breakfast Skillet	Avocado & Tuna Salad	Lemon Rosemary Grilled Chicken	Baked Peaches
44	Breakfast Tacos with Salsa	Lentil Soup	Black Bean Stuffed Peppers	Coconut & Almond Clusters
45	Cottage Cheese and Peach Bowl	Grilled Portobello Mushrooms	Cauliflower Fried Rice	Chocolate Dipped Orange Slices
46	Almond and Berry Granola	Spinach & Feta Stuffed Chicken	Lemon Butter Tilapia	Baked Apple Slices
47	Fruit Salad with Cinnamon	Shrimp & Veggie Stir Fry	Balsamic Glazed Chicken	Banana Ice Cream
48	Berry Smoothie	Baked Eggs with Spinach	Grilled Tuna Steaks	Greek Yogurt Popsicles

49	Almond Butter Toast	Cilantro Lime Chicken	Balsamic Glazed Salmon	Dark Chocolate Covered Strawberries
50	Overnight Oats with Berries	Pesto Chicken Salad	Garlic Herb Roasted Vegetables	Apple Cinnamon Muffins
51	Turkey and Avocado Wrap	Baked Cod with Veggies	Turkey Meatballs With Zoodles	Cocoa-Dusted Almonds
52	Buckwheat Pancakes	Chickpea Salad	Stuffed Acorn Squash	Baked Oatmeal with Berries
53	Vegetable Frittata	Spinach & Berry Salad	Grilled Lemon Herb Chicken	Vanilla Pudding with Berries
54	Turkey and Avocado Wrap	Tomato Basil Soup	Eggplant Rollatini	Coconut Macaroons
55	Avocado Egg Salad	Egg Salad Lettuce Wraps	Baked Cod with Veggies	Baked Peaches
56	Cottage Cheese with Pineapple	Bean and Veggie Soup	Garlic Shrimp Zoodle	Cocoa Avocado Mousse
57	Blueberry Protein Pancakes	Balsamic Veggie Bowl	Grilled Steak with Veggies	Pineapple Mint Sorbet
58	Whole Wheat Blueberry Pancakes	Turkey & Veggie Skillet	Spaghetti Squash Primavera	Dark Chocolate Covered Strawberries
59	Mushroom and Tomato Breakfast Skillet	Caprese Salad	Balsamic Glazed Chicken	Almond Flour Brownies
60	Spinach and Feta Wrap	Turkey Club Lettuce Wrap	Lemon Garlic Roasted Chicken	Raspberry Almond Bars

61	Quinoa Breakfast Bowl	Spinach & Berry Salad	Tofu Stir Fry	Apple Cinnamon Muffins
62	Avocado Egg Salad	Tomato Basil Soup	Stuffed Tomatoes	Greek Yogurt Popsicles
63	Tofu Scramble with Veggies	Egg Salad Lettuce Wraps	Baked Lemon Herb Chicken	Coconut Macaroons
64	Spinach and Mushroom Scramble	Bean and Veggie Soup	Grilled Steak with Veggies	Baked Oatmeal with Berries
65	Vegetable Frittata	Lentil Soup	Shrimp & Veggie Sautè	Vanilla Pudding with Berries
66	Blueberry Protein Pancakes	Turkey & Veggie Skillet	Eggplant Rollatini	Lemon Poppy Seed Muffins
67	Whole Wheat Blueberry Pancakes	Spinach & Quinoa Stuffed Peppers	Chicken Fajita Bowl	Cocoa Avocado Mousse
68	Mushroom and Tomato Breakfast Skillet	Caprese Salad	Grilled Salmon with Asparagus	Pineapple Mint Sorbet
69	Spinach and Feta Wrap	Tomato & Cucumber Salad	Herb Crusted Pork Tenderloin	Baked Peaches
70	Cottage Cheese with Pineapple	Grilled Chicken & Veggie Skewers	Black Bean Stuffed Peppers	Coconut & Almond Clusters

Conclusion

In conclusion, the GOLO diet is a popular and widely followed weight loss program that emphasizes the importance of balanced eating, steady blood sugar levels, and sustainable lifestyle changes. While there is limited scientific research specifically evaluating the effectiveness of the GOLO diet, many individuals have reported positive results in terms of weight loss and improved overall health. The key principles of the GOLO diet, such as consuming whole foods, managing portion sizes, and incorporating regular exercise, align with established principles of healthy eating and weight management. Additionally, the emphasis on stabilizing blood sugar levels through the use of the Release supplement is a unique aspect of this diet plan.

To get started on your GOLO journey, consider trying out the delicious and nutritious recipes included in this book. These recipes are designed to not only support your weight loss goals but also to make the process enjoyable and sustainable. Remember that the success of any diet plan ultimately depends on your commitment to making long-term lifestyle changes and finding the eating habits that work best for you. Enjoy the recipes, and may they contribute to your health and well-being.

"Enjoy The Journey!"

Index

Almond and Berry Granola; 30
Almond Butter Cookies; 65
Almond Butter Toast; 23
Almond Flour Brownies; 69
Apple and Cheese Slices; 89
Apple Cinnamon Muffins; 67
Apple Cinnamon Oatmeal; 29
Apple Slices with Almond Butter; 79
Avocado & Tuna Salad; 43
Avocado Egg Salad; 24
Baked Apple Slices; 64
Baked Cinnamon Apples; 75
Baked Cod with Veggies; 59
Baked Eggs with Spinach; 30
Baked Kale Chips; 81
Baked Lemon Herb Chicken; 50
Baked Oatmeal with Berries; 74
Baked Peaches; 72
Baked Pears with Cinnamon; 70
Baked Sweet Potato Fries; 87
Balsamic Glazed Chicken; 53
Balsamic Glazed Salmon; 61
Balsamic Veggie Bowl; 38
Banana Ice Cream; 71
Banana Nut Muffins; 25
Bean and Veggie Soup; 41
Berry Gelatin; 64
Berry Smoothie; 22
Black Bean Stuffed Peppers; 60
Blueberry Protein Pancakes; 33
Breakfast Tacos with Salsa; 33
Broccoli & Almond Salad; 46
Buckwheat Pancakes; 25
Caprese Salad; 40
Cauliflower Fried Rice; 55
Celery Sticks with Cream Cheese; 88
Cheese and Almond Plate; 81

Cheese and Turkey Roll Ups; 85
Cherry Tomatoes with Mozzarella; 83
Chicken Caesar Wrap; 39
Chicken Fajita Bowl; 52
Chickpea Salad; 47
Chocolate Dipped Orange Slices; 73
Chocolate Protein Balls; 75
Chocolate-Dipped Banana Slices; 76
Cilantro Lime Chicken; 58
Cocoa Avocado Mousse; 70
Cocoa-Dusted Almonds; 65
Coconut & Almond Clusters; 73
Coconut Macaroons; 69
Cottage Cheese and Peach Bowl; 32
Cottage Cheese with Pineapple; 27
Cottage Cheese with Sliced Cucumber; 82
Cucumber and Tomato Salad; 88
Dark Chocolate Covered Strawberries; 67
Edamame with Sea Salt; 86
Egg Salad Lettuce Wraps; 40
Eggplant Rollatini; 54
Frozen Banana Bites; 66
Fruit Salad with Cinnamon; 27
Garlic Herb Roasted Vegetables; 57
Garlic Shrimp Zoodle; 51
Greek Yogurt Popsicles; 66
Greek Yogurt with Berries and Honey; 90
Greek Yogurt with Nuts; 79
Grilled Chicken & Veggie Skewers; 42
Grilled Chicken Salad; 36
Grilled Eggplant Steaks; 62
Grilled Portobello Mushrooms; 45
Grilled Salmon with Asparagus; 52
Grilled Steak with Veggies; 50
Grilled Tuna Steaks; 56
Grilled Veggie Sandwich; 39
Hard-Boiled Eggs; 80

Herb Crusted Pork Tenderloin; 59
Lemon Butter Tilapia; 53
Lemon Garlic Roasted Chicken; 60
Lemon Poppy Seed Muffins; 71
Lemon Rosemary Grilled Chicken; 56
Lentil Soup; 44
Mediterranean Quinoa Salad; 36
Mixed Nuts; 82
Mushroom and Tomato Breakfast Skillet; 31
Overnight Oats with Berries; 24
Pesto Chicken Salad; 47
Pineapple Mint Sorbet; 74
Pumpkin Spice Muffins; 68
Quinoa Breakfast Bowl; 22
Raspberry Almond Bars; 72
Roasted Chickpeas; 78
Roasted Seaweed Sheets; 84
Sausage & Veggie Breakfast Skillet; 28
Shrimp & Veggie Sauté; 61
Shrimp & Veggie Stir Fry; 41
Spaghetti Squash Primavera; 51
Spiced Pumpkin Seeds; 80
Spinach & Berry Salad; 43
Spinach & Feta Stuffed Chicken; 48
Spinach and Feta Wrap; 29
Spinach and Mushroom Scramble; 23

Stuffed Acorn Squash; 55
Stuffed Mini Bell Peppers; 87
Stuffed Tomatoes; 57
Tofu Scramble with Veggies; 34
Tofu Stir Fry; 54
Tomato & Cucumber Salad; 45
Tomato Basil Soup; 42
Trail Mix with Nuts and Seeds; 89
Tuna Salad on Celery Sticks; 83
Tuna Salad Stuffed Avocado; 38
Turkey & Veggie Skillet; 46
Turkey and Avocado Wrap; 32
Turkey Club Lettuce Wrap; 37
Turkey Meatballs with Zoodles; 58
Vanilla Pudding with Berries; 68
Vegetable Frittata; 26
Veggie & Quinoa Stuffed Peppers; 44
Veggie Breakfast Burrito; 31
Veggie Sticks with Hummus; 78
Veggie Wrap; 37
Whole Grain Crackers with Cottage Cheese; 86
Whole Grain Rice Cakes with Avocado; 84
Whole Wheat Blueberry Pancakes; 28
Whole Wheat Pita with Tzatziki; 85
Zucchini Breakfast Muffins; 26

Made in the USA
Middletown, DE
25 June 2024